Echoes of the Ancient World

Series editor Werner Forman

BALI
The Split Gate to Heaven

BALI

The Split Gate to Heaven

Photographs by Werner Forman

Text by Rudolf Mrázek
and Bedřich Forman

Foreword by James A. Boon

ORBIS PUBLISHING · London

Note:
This book is concerned with traditional Balinese culture, as it
existed up until the twentieth century, and as it still exists in the villages of Bali
which are removed from the larger towns and tourist centres. The changes which
have been brought about in Bali as the result of its becoming a part of
the Dutch empire in 1908 and a part of the Republic of Indonesia,
and as a result of twentieth-century industrialization
and the influx of tourism, will not
be discussed.

Half-title page:
Left: Entrance dance of a noble hero. Right: The lotus represents
the cosmic focal point.

Title page:
A shadow-play puppet of Rangda, queen of witches. Her power is
so uncanny only a few puppeteers dared own or handle her. The puppets are held at a slant;
thus the shadows are sharp on top, increasingly diffused towards the bottom,
becoming even more eerily insubstantial. Bulaleng,
nineteenth century.

This page:
Every 210 days, at Galungan, Bali is adorned to honour the deified ancestor spirits
who descend to spend a few days with their kin.

Designed by Bedřich Forman

© 1983 Orbis Publishing Limited
First published in Great Britain by Orbis Publishing Limited, London 1983

Filmset in 'Monophoto' Bembo by Green Gates Studios, Hull, England
Printed in Singapore by TienWah Press (Pte.) Limited
ISBN 0-85613-513-5

CONTENTS

FOREWORD

This appealing study weaves together text and image to portray intricacies of Balinese society, history, art, politics, ritual, and worship. Rudolf Mrázek's essay is more than just another appreciation of Balinese lifestyle. It summarizes cultural forms and historical processes interpreted by anthropologists, philologists, artists and performers, and other scholars of the island's changing values and variations on traditional Indonesian patterns.

By skilfully selecting a sample of daily contexts, ritual events, folklore, legal regulations, chronicles, political tragedies, narratives, and drama, the author captures subtle flavours of Balinese life and performance. The intensity, ambition, comedy, and ambiguity of existence appear in the emotional tones of Bali-Hindu religious practices – from routine offerings, to ancestor commemoration, to trance. When Mrázek writes of 'pious' Balinese, readers should carefully note his explanation of *sayangang*, a term covering both the indulgence of a child and the worship of a deity. In Bali's style of 'piety' children are truly (playfully) regarded as gods, but so too are gods (in one manifestation) regarded as children, whose capricious desires must be satisfied, who must above all be entertained.

The book also reviews complex systems of irrigation control, local order, social status, and overlapping networks of influence and obligation. Even in their 'politics of vanity' the Balinese (like many Indonesian and Oceanic peoples) seem devoted more to rivalry than to outright domination, whether in traditional warfare, temple ceremonies, marriage arrangements, or cremations. The Balinese emphasize the dependence of the charismatic actor (or king) on his *audience*, which includes his underlings, his rivals, and his deities.

Observers of Bali have long sensed that the island's society is itself an aesthetic; lately we have increasingly realized that Balinese aesthetics conceal a sociology and a politics. This book succinctly demonstrates this fact by its choreography of comprehensive prose and pictorial splendour and detail. Moreover, the Formans' and Rudolf Mrázek's work shows that pictures can be essays and well-chosen words afford pictures; here it is difficult to say whether phrases caption photographs or photographs caption phrases. No interpretive format could be better suited to suggest the profound, constructive ambiguities behind the interrelation of the arts pervasive in Balinese civilization.

James A. Boon
Professor, Anthropology and Asian Studies, Cornell University

Rice, sweets and fruits of the land, offerings decorated with palm-leaf garlands and tassels, are brought to the temple on festival eve. The essence of the offerings is taken by the gods. What remains is taken home and consumed by the family. Nothing can be offered twice.

PROLOGUE

One of the thousands of islands which make up the Malay Archipelago, Bali is sandwiched between Java, to the west, and Lombok, to the east. Being less than ten degrees south of the equator, Bali has a tropical climate with only two seasons – rainy and dry, about equal in length. The Balinese see their island as a proud and daring cock. The backbone of the cock, and of the Balinese universe, is formed by the main ridge of the volcanic hill mass reaching across the island from east to west. The highest mountain in this volcanic chain is Gunung Agung, 'the navel of the world'. On the slopes of the mountains, Balinese civilization developed. Only the western part of the island – the raised tail of the cock – hilly, but without giant volcanoes, remains largely uncultured, barren, a buffer between Bali and the outside world, though not, it is true, a very effective one.

The best place to observe everyday life in Bali always was and still is on the open space of ground to be found at the main crossroads of almost every settlement. The atmosphere here is friendly and homely. Geese and ducks strut about arrogantly, heads high; people chat; girls seem to dance to and from the well, effortlessly balancing their heavy pottery jars full of water on their heads; children play. It is a scene of bustling serenity. There is almost always a huge banyan tree marking the site, providing shade for the central square of land, and for a huge area beyond. The banyan tree is holy, and is often used as a natural 'drum tower' containing the *kulkul*, or signal drum on which are beaten messages concerning village, or *desa*, and temple activities. It is a great umbrella, giving protection from sun and rain, and a fantastic playground for the children, a natural climbing frame. But in the evening, it sometimes becomes the haunt of dangerous spirits, or *leyaks*, and nobody would sleep near it for fear of going crazy.

Close by are the market, a cockfighting area, sometimes a *puri*, or palace, the home of some member of the aristocracy who happens to live in the village, and a temple or two. The temples, or *puras*, almost always have split gates.

There could hardly be a more dramatic contrast than that provided by the idyllic, peaceful, noisy, gay village common and the split gate, *candi bentar,* which looms up directly behind it. Taken by itself, the *candi bentar* is surely one of the most disquieting structures in the architecture of the world. It is derived from the ancient Indian and Javanese *candi,* the sanctuary where the ashes of the important and powerful were kept and worshipped. The monument still retains the *candi* shape but, in contrast to both India and Java, in Bali the *candi* is split. All the ornaments lovingly carved on the front and back of the *candi bentar* are mercilessly severed, cut through the middle of the smallest arabesque, and even through the middle of the grotesque face glaring from the top of the gate. The split gate is the passageway to the temple court, towards the gods, towards heaven. But there is a slash and something very pure and solemn seems to have been destroyed by it.

Outsiders tend to see the Balinese as almost unnervingly happy people. Yet every so often, a terrible volcanic eruption shakes the island and destroys large parts of it; There were three great ones in this century, in 1917, in 1926 and in 1963. The inexplicable violence of these eruptions, and of the sea, of monsoon storms and rains, which for six months in every year, from October to April, wreak sporadic havoc with the land, makes this paradise seem sometimes close to hell. The fertile soil of Bali is a product of volcanic ash, and monsoons are necessary – but contrasts are extreme, and paradoxes, even in nature, constitute the norm. And there are equally regular and equally shocking outbursts of social upheaval and violence, as, in this century, the *puputans* of 1906–8, and the bloodshed of 1965. The Balinese split gate, leading into the temple, may be seen as a symbol of this ambivalence, as the demons' guarded way to heaven.

Above: A small rice offering decorated by a flower cut out of a palm leaf, on the ground near the netherworld temple at Bratan, in an area where one deity is believed to be Chinese, and thus enjoys opium, fireworks and chopsticks for his food.

Right: A banyan tree near Pejeng. Kulkuls (signal blocks) are sometimes hung on the trees, which thus become like village bell-towers.

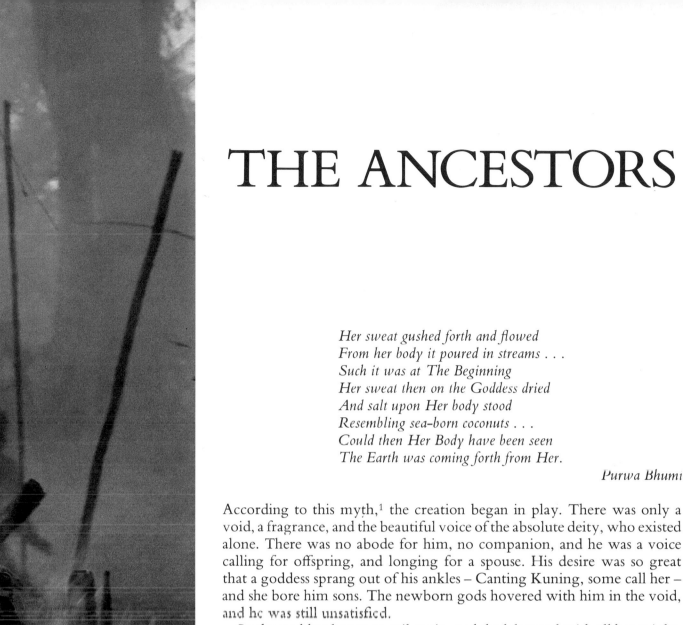

THE ANCESTORS

Her sweat gushed forth and flowed
From her body it poured in streams . . .
Such it was at The Beginning
Her sweat then on the Goddess dried
And salt upon Her body stood
Resembling sea-born coconuts . . .
Could then Her Body have been seen
The Earth was coming forth from Her.

Purwa Bhumi

According to this myth,[1] the creation began in play. There was only a void, a fragrance, and the beautiful voice of the absolute deity, who existed alone. There was no abode for him, no companion, and he was a voice calling for offspring, and longing for a spouse. His desire was so great that a goddess sprang out of his ankles – Canting Kuning, some call her – and she bore him sons. The newborn gods hovered with him in the void, and he was still unsatisfied.

So the goddess began to toil again, and she laboured with all her might. Her sweat made the Holy River flow, and pervaded the space, giving it a resplendent hue. She remained in labour. Next, she brought forth the ocean and the earth. Then she looked up, and saw the sun, moon, and planets, and all the stars. A feverish heat flushed through her veins, and to cool her limbs the wind was created. The egg of the universe was given life.

At that time, the earth was the width of a single turf, and the sky just matched a sunshade's width. But soon, the primordial god made mountains and forests and fields, birds and serpents, sharks and sawfish, until earth, sky and sea were full of life. Then he fashioned man out of clay, and gave the world to him.

The world soon became crowded. Men were being thoughtlessly created. They wandered through the forest, mated anywhere, abandoned their children, lived and ate like beasts. The supreme being, observing them, felt lonely again, and distressed at the way he had peopled the world. One version of the story has it that while he was lost in despair, he released a drop of semen by mistake. It dropped to earth, and out of it a giant devil was born. The devil became known on earth as 'the inspirer of fear', 'the shadow on the ground', 'the shadow on the

A whole inheritance is often consumed in an effort to purify the soul of the dead and revitalize it for its eventual return to earth.

Above: Pura Sada, desa Kapal, probably sixteenth-century.

Below: Wisnu, at the back of the lotus throne, astride his giant bird, Garuda. The lowest part of the padmasana is represented by the devil's head. The top is divided into three thrones for Brahma, Siwa and Wisnu.

Right: Krishna. Detail from a scroll said to be a Wayang scroll. As he unwinds it, the dalang (puppeteer) tells the story.

water', 'the shadow in the mirror'. Men began to fear one another. Fear fed on fear.

Some say the devil was the fearful Kbo Iwa who, in anguish, carved with his fingernails the mountains and caves near Batur Lake. Kbo Iwa was awe-inspiring and strangely moving in appearance. His long tusks radiated like drops of dew, his eyes stared like suns, his nostrils were deep as wells, and his mouth gaped like a cavern. His voice was a scream of pain, and the poor monster was driven by an insatiable desire to devour mankind. He trapped men on the roads, hunted them through ravines and forests, and drove lonely creatures towards the mountains or the sea. Even the animals were filled with pity at the sight of men fleeing in fright.

Soon corpses were heaped mountain high, and blood flowed in a torrent from the hills. Mankind had almost ceased to exist on earth. The time for play was over, and the gods themselves were appalled and frightened. They hurled weapons at the devil, but every time a weapon pierced him, he was made stronger by it. Then they tried persuasion, but that did not work either, and they only just escaped being devoured themselves. Finally, according to one version of the myth, a sorely tormented human being stood up, and declared an end to the carnage. The man (perhaps a god in disguise) quietened the demon by telling him that he must go away, but that he was welcome to return any time he wished to stay with men, and to consume anyone who still deserved to be eaten. He could make a meal of those men whom he caught sleeping at noon, or leaving their houses during the night without singing or having quarrelled, or anyone roaming about on the crossroads, or lazing in the fields, or being arrogant in the temples, and he could eat any child unlucky enough to be born in the *tumpek wayang* week. The man/god invited the demon to remain close by, and to keep his mouth open. And he did not forget to teach his fellow men how to live properly, so that they could escape the demon's jaws.

The story of creation is told in countless forms, repeated again and again. The elements of creation, rampaging fear and civilization following one upon the other make this myth authentically Balinese. For the drama, creation and fear, destruction and renewal, is still always happening in Bali. It is the cycle following a volcanic eruption; it is also a cycle which the Balinese have experienced in many other forms, social, political and spiritual, throughout their history.

Praying to their ancestors, the Balinese have always looked away from the sea. The Balinese locate the land of their uncivilized ancestors in the middle of the island, in the mountains, or in the deserted and wild jungles of the west.[2] The beauty of the beaches never moved them; the sea has always been a realm of horror – the home of the spirits of the netherworld, and battleground of witches. One woman, who lived in the coastal village of Sanur, was said on occasional nights to turn into a witch, or *leyak*, and then into a beam of light, which waged war against another beam of light on the sea. Several Balinese say they have seen her in this form. And as recently as 1981, it was claimed that the terrible rats in the ricefields near the sea were in fact fish that came to wreak havoc on the land at night.

It still does not matter to the Balinese that, according to some modern scholars, many of the fundamentals of Balinese culture came from across the seas. The ancestors of the Balinese race may have come from mainland Asia, from the semitropical interior of southern China,[3] where they must have revered their gods and forefathers, and mountains, rocks and stones, the abodes of deities. They had already mastered the art of shaping sharp and exquisitely refined and polished stone implements, had cleared

the jungle, and possibly knew how to irrigate their fields. Between 10,000 and 5000 B C, either in a spirit of adventure or perhaps out of fear of an enemy stronger than themselves, they began to move south, towards the coastal plains. When they reached the coast of China, they built canoes and made many ventures out across the sea.

Eventually they found Bali, green but wild. We know nothing of what happened next, but clearly the newcomers worked hard on the land, for after several thousand years had passed the island was cultivated and humanized. The jungle was cleared now along the coast and far up the hillside; irrigated terraces of ricefields were built where previously forests had stretched. The valleys and hillsides displayed those light and elegant pavilion-type houses, *balés*, that are still so typical of the Balinese landscape. Smiths, stoneworkers and carpenters were hard at work in the compounds. The profusion of bronze tools, delicate bronze ornaments and imposing kettle-drums which these people produced showed fine craftsmanship. Holy stones were dressed up brightly during festive occasions, and long *lamaks*, patterned banners plaited from the yellow and green leaves of coconut and sugar-palm, hung from tall, swaying, bamboo poles. Cockfights were already held in *wantilans* or cockfighting rings, the *gamelan selunding*, or orchestra with iron keys, and the *angklung*, or bamboo orchestra, played, and perhaps rudimentary forms of *sangh-yang,* trance dances, and *kecak,* male choruses, were already enjoyed.[4]

A Chinese Buddhist monk, traveller, and author of one of the earliest and most confusing reports on Southeast Asia,[5] might have been mistaken, or we might have misunderstood him. The 'Kingdom of P'o-li' he visited may or may not be the island of Bali. But wherever he was, many of the features he describes fit the Bali which archaeologists believe to have existed by the sixth century A D. Obviously it was at that time, as it is now, 'a warm island of luxurious vegetation and of fertile soil giving as much as two harvests a year'. And it is quite possible that there may have already been as many as 136 villages, as reported by the monk, and even that a Hindu king, who prided himself on being the direct descendant of the Buddha's father, and who professed the Hindu faith, welcomed visitors.

Very early indeed, and probably by the sixth century, when the monk was writing, Balinese life began to be rearranged according to a new religion coming also from overseas. The Hindu creed gradually changed the Balinese landscape. Holy grounds and *balés* of Balinese chiefs were walled in, gates were built in the walls, and images of Hindu gods were created, perhaps already by the sixth century. In place of magic stones, shrines were erected and *merus*, pagoda-like temple roofs, were built as new symbols of the holy Balinese mountains. Sometime during this period, Brahmanic priests came to Bali and established themselves inside the new *puris*, or palaces. Some may have come direct from India, and others perhaps from one of the Hinduized countries of Southeast Asia, either invited by the Balinese chiefs or left behind by merchant ships sailing between India and China. They brought their conch shells and their religion, Hindu legal books for the chiefs and Hindu manuals on how to rule and how to collect taxes. New genealogies were inscribed by the priests, linking Balinese chiefs with the Hindu gods, and with the heroes of the Hindu epics, the *Ramayana* and the *Mahabharata*. The Balinese chiefs took on new titles, *raja, ratu, prabu, cokorda,* and from that time they were kings and princes. Also around that time, the first of them was cremated in the Hindu way.

A new history of Bali was created by the Hindu priests. The island was described as being barren and flat before the holy mountains were brought by the gods from India. Then a coconut flower, growing wild on the

Details of a cloth painting from Kamasan, second half of the twentieth century. Cloth paintings of this sort are used as curtains at the side of a couch in a ritual pavilion or a temple. Here, the subjects depicted indicate that it might have been used during a marriage ceremony.

Below: The nymph Supraba seduces the demon king Niwatakawaca.

Right: Arjuna playing with a nymph.

mountain slopes, was blessed by the Indian gods, and twins were born of the flower, a boy and a girl, who married and became Bali's first king and queen.

New teaching was also superimposed on the original creation myth: now it was considered to have been the goddess Uma, Siwa's wife, who had, in the beginning, delivered Bali in sweat and pain, and the demon who was born to devour human beings appeared to be none other than the god Kala, Siwa's son. Siwa himself was the sun, and it was the sacred duty of the Balinese from now on to work for him and pray to him.

The Brahmanic priests long remained strangers in Bali. They haughtily kept aloof from others and people watched them with suspicion (as indeed, to some extent they do to this day). But slowly, contacts between the new culture and the people multiplied. Hindu music was heard through the palace walls, and dancers from the villages were asked to learn Hindu dance patterns and to perform them for the king. Hindu musical instruments were accepted by village orchestras if their sound was considered delightful enough. Hindu dances, myths, dramas, if found exciting, were included in peasants' dramatic performances. Hindu gods, if charming, were married to Balinese ancestors, and cremation – its Hindu form changed beyond recognition – was added to the traditional Balinese ceremonies.

The legend described the original Balinese royal twins who came out of the blessed coconut as beautiful creatures, who loved each other and

Above: Cloth painting. Kamasan, twentieth century. 'Bhima Swarga', the story of a 'Mahabharata' hero's visit to hell, is almost always told on the eve of a cremation. Wicked souls are described being tortured by infernal beings. But at the end the hero always comes out of hell unscathed. Below: Cloth painting. The churning of the ocean by gods and demons.

Above: The netherworld depicted on the black sandstone carving of Pura Beji at Sangsit. The world turtle Bedawang 'Nala is being held by two mythical snakes. The Balinese supplement the Hindu myth with an explanation of their own: the reason the snakes' embrace is so tight is because they must keep the turtle from moving too violently and causing another catastrophic earthquake.

ruled a tranquil realm. About their descendants, the Balinese kings, and the dynasties of the dimly lit past before the eleventh century, we do not even know that much. A few names are preserved, but details of their history are unknown, and even the broad outlines are largely forgotten, or overlaid in myth. One of the few things that is remembered from the time of the earliest inscriptions is that Java, the large island to the west, loomed on the horizon across the narrow Bali Strait.

Already, the mythical 'first' in the Javanese royal genealogy, King Sanjaya, named in an inscription of AD 732, is said to have conquered and subjected the island of Bali as well as Sumatra and even Cambodia, India and China. The oldest dated inscription found in Bali is only from AD 882. The first king ruling in Bali and known by name was Ugrasena (c. 915-42), the founder of the Warmadewa dynasty. Three kings and a queen of largely forgotten merits followed Ugrasena. Buddhism and Siwaism had been introduced to the country, and Pura Besakih, on the slopes of Gunung Agung, became the dynasty's state temple. An embassy was sent to the Chinese imperial court. Bali was apparently independent then, but Java remained by far the greatest outside influence.

Late in the tenth century, Bali was conquered again, very efficiently it seems, by the eastern Javanese king, Dharmawangsa (989-1007). He subdued the island, sent his sister (or maybe sister-in-law), Princess Mahendradatta, there, and had her placed on the throne beside (or rather above) the Balinese king.

Java was eternally present in Bali, like the tidal waves which submerged the island's shores, receded, and came again. Great Erlangga (1019-49), son of Mahendradatta, was born in Bali, married a Javanese princess, became a king in Java and made Bali part of his Javanese empire. Before he died, his Javanese realm was divided, then plundered, and Bali was left free. By the early twelfth century, a new eastern Javanese kingdom of Kediri reached its zenith, and Bali was listed among its fifteen vassals. By 1222 Kediri, after a century of glory, was defeated by the founder of Singhasari, another Javanese state, and Bali is described as being independent again – until the greatest of the Singhasari kings, Kertanegara, set his eyes on the island: 'In bodies-sky-suns Shaka [*i.e.* 1284] he sent men yonder to the land of Bali, to be subjugated. Without delay its Ratu [queen] was overpowered; made a captive she came to the Prince according to custom' (*Nagara-kertagama* – Javanese text of AD 1365).

From around the time Mahendradatta is believed to have settled in Bali, Javanese, instead of Old Balinese, became the real language of the Balinese court and the official language of the kingdom. The early Hindu era in Bali merged into Hindu-Javanese, and ancient tales describe how the Javanese holy men acquired such strength and agility that they could fly 'riding on a leaf' across the Bali Strait.

The Javanese kings between the eighth and thirteenth century counted among the most aggressive rulers in the vast area between India and China. Yet at the same time Javanese literature, architecture and sculpture reveal one of the richest, most exciting cultures in the world. The magnificent Siwaist temples of Dieng Plateau, the immense Buddhist stupa, Borobudur, and the delightful Lara-Jonggrang temple group of Prambanan were all built during that time, and by those warlike kings. Dharmawangsa, Javanese aggressor, conqueror of Bali, the Terrible Lord, is said to have been at the same time a great enlightener, setting scribes to translate and copy great parts of the Indian epic, *Mahabharata*, for the first time in an Indonesian language.

The Javanese priests added new shrines, walls and gates to the holiest temple in Bali, Besakih, on the slopes of the Gunung Agung. They built magnificent new Balinese temples at Goa Lelawah, Gelgel, Sasih and Pejeng. The Javanese style of sculpture and architecture strongly influenced the Balinese and the temples and palaces of Bali were rebuilt and redecorated in the Javanese manner. The esoteric art of classical Java was assimilated with Bali's raw, earthy forms, creating a more delicate style, one that many people find more expressive and richer than either Balinese or Javanese art had been before. Bali was not merely conquered by Java; Bali was enchanted by the conquerors.

And all this was still before the high point of Javanese influence in Bali. By 1292, Kertanegara was dead, his kingdom destroyed, and rulers installed (or reinstalled) in Bali who, from everything we know about them, did not show a hint of political dependence on any other country. Only two years after Kertanegara died, however, a new Javanese kingdom of Majapahit was founded. In 1305, according to tradition, a Majapahit king entered into a mystic union with four princesses, representatives of the four countries which recognized Majapahit supremacy, one of which was Bali. Early in the fourteenth century, the Majapahit chief minister, Gajah Mada, took a solemn oath that he would not enter the temple until Java, was restored to the greatness of her imperial past. Accordingly, soon, Bali was attacked:

'. . . in the Shaka year arrows-seasons-eyes-navel [1343] that Bali there, its Protectors were all evil-disposed, vile. Aimed at by an expedition of the Royal servants, they were exterminated, all of them destroyed. Awed were all kinds of evil-doers, retiring, running away'.

Nagara-kertagama

It happened so often. Javanese conquerors came and went. Following the death in 1389 of Hayam Wuruk, the greatest of the Majapahit kings, the Javanese imperialism began to recede from Bali again. But, as far as Bali was concerned, this time the backlash seemed stronger than the wave.

Throughout the dramatic decades of the fifteenth century, as the glorious Majapahit period was nearing its end (largely due to the mounting power of Islam coming from the Middle East), the Javanese Majapahit

Bali still wild and untamed. A scene near Lake Buyan.

Pura Ulun Siwi, an ancient temple at the narrow isthmus connecting the island with the southern Bukit peninsula. Unlike most Balinese temples, here are no meru-like structures, but only huge boulders. Stone seats are still clothed at this temple and worshipped as during pre-Hindu times. More such temples are situated in the interior, some of them virtually deserted, for the Balinese say the stones in them are so powerful that it is not safe to approach them if one does not know exactly how to worship the spirits connected with the place.

élite started more and more to gravitate towards the small island just to the east. Bali, in the fourteenth century only one of countless subject territories, gradually emerged as the only conceivable place for the Javanese royalty to escape to. As tradition has it, the last prince of Majapahit, unable to withstand the Muslim pressure, crossed the Bali Strait in 1478 with all his regalia, priests, courtiers and dancers. What a strange procession it would have been. Overrefined, nostalgic, bitter – a ruler without a realm, captains without an army, priests without temples, artists – all without a motherland. They set out to find what they had lost in Bali, or to create it anew.

First, a new myth had to be invented to explain their arrival and to legitimize their stay. The Balinese story of creation was remodelled, now in a Majapahit version. 'In the beginning was Majapahit; what lies before it is a chaos of demons and villains about which the Balinese knows practically nothing.'[6] Bali was a barren, flat island before a holy man of Majapahit, Mpu Kulputih, decided to pray for the improvement of the land. The god Pasupati answered his prayers by sending his children to Bali, along with a part of the mountain of the gods, which became the holiest Gunung Agung. Another Majapahit seer, Nirartha, then wandered the length and breadth of Bali and lay with native women of all classes. He begot a daughter, Sri Melanting, the Balinese goddess of gardens and dry fields, and a number of sons, ancestors of all the priests yet to be born in Bali. Sang Kepakisan, another blessed man of Majapahit, practised ascesis and acquired thus the power to beget out of stone the father of the first

22

Balinese king – which is to say, the first king virtuous enough to be accepted by Javanese overlords.[7]

The Balinese rulers and nobility who had survived the conquest now hurriedly began to find ways of joining their family trees with Majapahit ministers and captains and priests. *Bali-aga*, 'original Balinese' became a despised appellation and whoever wanted to be respected in Bali actually started calling himself *Wong Majapahit*, 'Man of Majapahit', and many do still today. The cultured and proudly self-contained Balinese accepted readily, even eagerly, another story of creation, another way of life brought by conquerors coming from overseas. It was not for the first time, and just as before, the apparent paradox was solved by the Balinese in an elegant way.

The Majapahit culture in Bali was both magnificent and touching, particularly in its decline at the time of the fifteenth century when it ceased to be an official culture of the empire and became rather a displaced culture on the run. Hardly anything in Bali remained untouched, unmoved by this Javanese swell. Almost everything of cultural value, magical content, spiritual power, was, and still is, affectionately guarded and explicitly described by the Balinese as an 'heirloom of Majapahit'. The *kris* (dagger) and all the other kinds of weaponry, many kinds of *gamelan* music, *wayang* (shadow-play puppets) and many genres of theatre, *legong* and many of the delicate dances – everything that 'came from Majapahit' was eagerly and respectfully accepted by the Balinese, and changed beyond recognition. The Javanese conquest was absorbed, and turned into a powerful manifestation of classical Balinese culture.

A shrine for *Batara Majapahit*, the teachers of Majapahit, can be found in nearly every Balinese temple, and there are hundreds of finely carved deer heads, or antlers, symbols of Majapahit, revered throughout the island. Since the fifteenth century, the Balinese have thought of Majapahit as their culture-origin centre, but the great majority of them knew only vaguely what the name stood for, either historically or geographically. The 'Majapahit deer' was to them just a good-natured animal who gave suck to a legendary Balinese king when he was left in the woods as a tiny baby. Gajah Mada, the Majapahit minister who planned the Balinese conquest, is still presented in the traditional Balinese drama as having been born of a coconut flower, as the original Balinese twins were. Kulputih, Kepakisan and Nirartha may have ridden a leaf across the strait from Java, but surely they ascended to the Balinese heaven long ago, and joined forces there with all the other Balinese ancestors.

In 1290, four years before the Majapahit dynasty was founded, the first town in Indonesia was converted to Islam. Two centuries later the new creed had become a major power in the area, submerging Malaya, Sumatra, and the whole of Java, reaching eastward to the utmost limits of the vast archipelago.

> Blambangan, weak in itself, was vigorously supported by the warlike Balinese who . . . firmly resisted Mataram's attempt to extend its authority over the coastlands opposite Bali. Their resistance against Javanese political domination made the Balinese hold on to their ancient social structure . . . [Sultan Agung] undertook the conquest of the eastern territory and of Bali in 1639. Blambangan was quickly overrun. Mataram's troops then crossed the narrow straits between Java and Bali but the Balinese put up such a fierce resistance that the conquest of the island could not be completed.[8]

Bali controlled some areas of eastern Java until late in the eighteenth

A kendang player – a member of the famous gambuh orchestra that used to adorn the Sukawati palace. This base of a balé pillar, carved out of volcanic tuff, dates from the sixteenth or seventeenth century. To this day the kendang drum is used as one of the most important instruments to direct the rhythm and structure of the ancient baris and topeng performances, as well as the modern kebyar.

Gunung Kawi, 'poet's mountain', on the east side of River Pakerisan near Tampaksiring. Some of the very few candis still to be found in Bali, these five are believed to have been carved in the rock by the fearful demon Kbo Iwa in pre-Majapahit times. The inscription on the largest of the candis was interpreted as 'the king who is interred in Yalu'. The youngest son of King Udayana and brother of the great Erlangga, Anak Wungsu, ruler of Bali between 1046 and 1077, is thought to be the one referred to in the inscription. The other four candis perhaps cover the ashes of the king's four wives who died on the funeral pyre.

century, the island of Sumbawa for a time, and part of Lombok right up to the end of the nineteenth century. In those centuries, the Balinese became famed throughout Indonesia for their warlike nature, and their indifference to death; Bali was even called the 'stronghold' against Mohammedanism.[9] She fought to keep herself free to absorb the Majapahit impact, to develop and perfect a culture of her own. Islam has always been a threat to Bali – but it was never allowed to become anything more. And as the Islamic wave that completely changed the island world between India and China was avoided by the Balinese, for a long time it seemed that the Dutch wave that followed would be avoided too.

The first ships from that faraway Christian country approached Bali's shores as early as 1597, but rather by accident than through any preconceived plan.[10] The three ships, owned by Cornelis de Houtman, an Amsterdam merchant, had actually headed in a quite different direction, and only after many sailors, a captain and a ship were lost in a skirmish near Java was the original idea abandoned. Frustrated, the Dutch had decided to return home, and it was then that they found Bali. After nine weeks, early in 1598, the sailors left the island. Later that year, the ships' logs, kept by Houtman, were published, and they caused a sensation in Holland.

There was almost everything in the journals, bright colours, lovely women, but no mention of spices, and that was what counted to mercantile sixteenth-century Europe.

Bali did export slaves, and they made a very good price in Asian markets at that time. Bali also exported pork, and she imported gold and precious stones to embellish court dancers, musical instruments and royal weapons. But this trade was not promising enough to encourage the Europeans to take the trouble to attack Bali's difficult coasts and warlike people. The Dutchmen, of course, came again – in fact the Dutch cleared eastern Java of the Balinese in the eighteenth century – but they did not assault the Balinese heartland, and whoever approached them in the seventeenth and eighteenth centuries and proposed a common campaign against the island always received more or less the same answer: the Dutch still did not want to be involved.

Houtman's pitiful flotilla started a new era elsewhere in the eastern archipelago. The Dutchmen's East India Company was safely settled there by the late seventeenth century, and by the middle of the eighteenth century, only a very few of the Indonesian islands remained free from the interference of the Dutch. Bali was one of the few.

Divine gate-keepers at a tiny family temple clothed for a festival. The magically potent black and white chequered cloth they wear is believed in this particular case to empower the guardians to ward off from the temple women at the time of menses, coarse outsiders, and other unwelcome guests.

27

On 22 November 1815, the Tambora volcano erupted on the island of Sumbawa, and the gigantic wave caused by the blast reached Bali almost immediately. The sea was convulsed, the skies were black above the island for three days, and as the heavy showers of ash fell, roofs collapsed. The earth quivered, and stormy rain beat down on the mountains. Torrents of mud, four metres deep, poured down the slopes, through the valleys and ricefields, towards the sea. Buleleng and Singaraja, the two largest towns of northern Bali, were badly damaged, and more than ten thousand people were swept away by the flood. Plague and famine followed.

A calamity of this nature strikes Bali about once in a lifetime, and is always taken by the Balinese as a punishment or a premonition. After the eruption, terrible things were expected, and everybody knew they would come from the sea. Hardly anyone guessed, however – even at that late date – that the next disaster would be caused by the Dutch.

In 1817, a Dutch official arrived in Bali to discuss commerce seriously with the Balinese rulers for the first time. He was not too successful, but ships loaded with pork and gold, cotton, rice, coffee, corn, tobacco, salt, cattle, fowl, fruit and opium began to multiply in Balinese waters. Singaraja recovered from the flood and, along with Kuta in the south, burgeoned into a busy port. In 1826, a permanent Dutch representative

Left: Jayapangus's edict, one of a set of bronze plates inscribed in old Javanese script in AD 1181. It deals with community regulations.

settled in Kuta not far from the royal palace of Badung. European interest in Bali grew, the first Dutch-Bali treaties were signed, and the first promises on both sides were broken. The limits of intervention were more sharply defined, and the temptation to transgress them increased.

In 1841 a Dutch vessel ran aground on the Balinese coast and, according to an ancient custom, was accepted by the Balinese king as a gift from the gods. This was not the first time that a European ship had ended up as a 'gift', but times were changing, and Bali was deemed due for punishment. Three 'punitive expeditions' quickly followed, during the monsoon of 1846, in 1848 and in 1849. Fleets of frigates, steamships, schooners, land forces of thousands of Indonesians, hundreds of European mercenaries, field artillery, and horses were deployed. It was the strongest force that had ever been used against natives of the Indonesian archipelago.[11] Jagaraga, in Buleleng, fell to the Dutch in 1849.

Bali was in turmoil and it is difficult to say whether this was the traditional state of Balinese political life or a hysteria inspired by mounting pressure from the Dutch. Dewa Agung, *raja* of Klungkung and king of Bali, was the ruler of the whole island only in name. Bali was divided – and probably had been for a long time – into several largely independent kingdoms, each with its own conception of freedom. Frequently, they banded together to protect that freedom against an external threat. But even more often, they warred among themselves, and nothing could have helped the Dutch more to attain their ultimate aim.

Less than a decade after Jagaraga fell, in 1855 and 1856, the northern Balinese kingdom of Buleleng and the western kingdom of Jembrana were forced to accept Dutch controllers, their advice and 'protection'.

One of the temples of Ubud. The covered gate is adorned for the festival. The closed door signals that the gods are not yet present.

Walls are a significant part of the Balinese temples. They keep the sacred territory safe from evil influence, often by portraying figures that are charged with evil force themselves. But comedy is present too.

Top: technology comes to Bali: the back wheel is a lotus bloom, and the gear-wheel's teeth are curved as though the cyclist is moving backwards. Above: the intruders, penises are devilishly huge, but the attacked and molested women seem content. (The top relief is from Pura Meduwe Karang, the second from a netherworld temple at Sangsit, Buleleng.)

Two years later, a Balinese 'proposed' by the Dutch was put on the Buleleng throne. In 1882, both Buleleng and Jembrana were brought under direct Dutch rule. All Balinese women in that part of the island were ordered by an official decree to cover their breasts, in order to protect the morals of the Dutch soldiers. Blouse-wearing became a fashion, and spread from those Dutch-protected enclaves throughout the island, as a forewarning of what was soon to follow.

The eastern Balinese kingdom of Karangasem and the part of the island of Lombok which was dominated by Karangasem were subjugated by the Dutch in 1894. By that time, another kingdom, Mengwi, on the southern slopes of the central Balinese mountain ridge, had been defeated, but in this case the attack had come from Mengwi's aggressive Balinese neighbours. In 1899 the kingdom of Gianyar, east of Mengwi, similarly threatened by the united forces of the kingdom of Tabanan, Badung, Bangli and Klungkung, turned for help to – of all choices – the Dutch, received protection, and was annexed in due course. Now the Dutch were well and truly inside the Balinese heartland, and only four of the orginally nine Balinese kingdoms were left to stop their advance.

Again a wrecked ship, a Chinese schooner, served as the pretext for war – this time, for the decisive battle. On 14 September, 1906, the Sixth Military Expedition, according to Dutch count, landed on Bali, on the beautiful southern beach at Sanur; it was larger than any that had gone before. The Balinese marched on the strangers with spears and *krises*, some golden. The Dutch retorted with guns. The Balinese retreated, and a Dutch brass band entertained any who remained to listen with Western love songs. It sounds like an operetta, but the scene was set for tragedy. On the morning of 20 September, the Dutch column proceeding inland moved against the royal palace of Badung, just two hours' march away.

For the Dutch soldiers, this was merely another battle in rounding off the empire. For the Balinese, it was the *puputan* – the end, the destruction.

They met the enemy a few hundred metres from the palace gate, where the main avenue of Denpasar is today:

The Dutch troops, marching in orderly ranks along the long roadway, walled on either side, which led to the royal palace, were not surprised to find the town apparently deserted and flames and smoke rising over the *puri*, the most disquieting factor being the sound of the wild beating of drums within the palace walls. As they drew closer, they observed a strange, silent procession emerging from the main gate of the *puri*. It was led by the Raja himself, seated in his state palanquin carried by four bearers, dressed in white cremation garments but splendidly bejewelled and armed with a magnificent *kris*. The Raja was followed by the officials of his court, the armed guards, the priests, his wives, his children, and his retainers, likewise dressed in white, flowers in their hair, many of them almost as richly ornamented and as splendidly armed as the Raja himself.

One hundred paces from the startled Dutch, the Raja halted his bearers, stepped from his palanquin, gave the signal, and the ghastly ceremony began. A priest plunged his dagger into the Raja's breast, and others of the company began turning their daggers upon themselves or upon one another. The Dutch troops, startled into action by a stray gunshot and reacting to attack by lance and spear, directed rifle and even artillery fire into the surging crowd. Some of the women mockingly threw jewels and gold coins to the soldiers, and as more and more persons kept emerging from the palace gate, the mounds of corpses rose higher and higher. Soon to the scene of carnage was added the spectacle of looting as the soldiers stripped the valuables from the corpses and then set themselves to sacking the palace ruins.[12]

More than 3500 people died during the Badung *puputan*. Two days later, the *raja* of the neighbouring kingdom of Tabanan killed his son and then plunged a *sirih* knife (a tiny knife used for whittling a combination of plants, nuts and spices, for chewing) into his own throat. Two frenzied years passed, the Dutch attacked the sole remaining independent *raja*, the *raja* of Klungkung, paramount lord of Bali, and the Balinese embarked on their final *puputan*. Through it, on 18 April, 1908, the last independent Balinese kingdom, and some say classical Bali itself, came to an end.

Balinese history is trying and sometimes frustrating for anyone who studies it. *Lontars* (palm-leaf books) are fragile, and do not last long. The histories, or *babads*, inscribed in them are copied and recopied, mistakes creep in, the past is misused and forgotten, the actors are faceless, abstract, with borrowed names and predictable deeds. Time is vague, chronology collapses. The *babads* kept in temples are believed to be endowed with magic powers, and when the histories are recited by the priest, everybody accepts them as the words of the gods.[13] But they are not intended to facilitate an accurate reconstruction of the past. Not, at least, in a sense we would call historically logical.

As one of the greatest Dutch scholars wrote in 1949, 'Everywhere in Bali, history has deep roots, though it rarely leaves clear traces.'[14] The Balinese *paras* (stone) is moist and soft and melts away in a few centuries. The temples built of *paras* – and most are in part – seem almost alive; they are only considered to be 'real' while they are being incessantly improved, repaired, or built anew. The frequently cited comparison of Bali to a sculptor's studio fittingly describes the permanent state of flux which exists there, and which is considered right. The very symbol of 'permanency of settlement' in some traditional villages is a shrine inside the soft-stone *pura puseh,* or temple of origin, deliberately constructed of even more transitory material – abodes for the gods of woven bamboo supported by the sprouting branches of a *dapdap* tree.[15] Ancient things are not revered in Bali so much as things living, dying, and emerging again – for these are what represent the 'reality of the present' and 'the reality of the past' for the Balinese.

Bali has been subdued repeatedly by invasions of strangers. The devils, the terrible Kbo Iwa, Kala and Rangda (the witch seen often as a personification of Mahendradatta, the Javanese conquering princess) kept emerging to devour the people (or sometimes to turn them into wild banana flowers), and destroy their island. Still today, they come in such personifications as the *kalas* and *butas*, minor demons irresistibly drawn to almost every festival or ceremony. They may dance, or just be felt to be present. They are absolutely real to the Balinese, and they are essential; without them the drama of creation, fear and civilization could not be performed.

Even the *puputans* of 1906-8 could be viewed, in a sense, as performances. Bali trembled whenever the time came for *puputan*. But perhaps the *puputans* were also considered the right move in time of deepest crisis: if they failed, at least they destroyed all that preceded them. The *puputans* of 1906 and 1908 were surely performed in despair and self-destructive fury, but perhaps also in the belief that only thus a path towards renewal would be cleared.

Kris handle of ivory, gold and precious stones. Danganan, eighteenth century. The rulers of Majapahit are said to have brought their divine krises and palaces with them to Bali.
The power of the ancestors accumulates in krises which become the most sacred family heirlooms kept in temples, and gods like to enter them during festivals. There were taboos regarding the royal krises, especially against a foreigner touching them. The noblest of these krises were broken during puputans.

THE HEIRS

He stretches his hands over the incense smoke, uncovers the tray in front of him, and mumbles the mantra asta mantra, the hand-cleansing formula, rubs the palms of his hands with a flower and sandalwood powder, 'wiping out impurity', and recites a formula for each finger as it is passed over the palm of each hand, taking flowers which he holds over the incense smoke and then flinging them away saying: 'Be happy, be perfect, be glad in your heart'.[1]

The sheer will to survive shaped the bright and delicately refined people we still meet in the villages of the island. More than two thousand years ago, close to extinction or animal subsistence, their ancestors snatched from the jungle the soil the jungle had swallowed up from the volcanoes; changed the course of rivers on their way from the mountains to the sea, and made them irrigate the fields.

The jungle still stretches close to the volcanoes' summits. Lower, the first clearing can be seen, the first settlements, dry fields, a water conduit and an irrigated field. Here, dams are a rare sight. The people of the mountains – called *Bali-aga,* or original Balinese – have maintained simple and stern customs, and they still subsist largely on maize, sweet potatoes, and other crops given by non-irrigated fields. Lower down the slopes is the home of about eighty per cent of the island's population – the Balinese heartland. The jungle is cleared. The rivers are dammed, and irrigation is so thorough that there is not – as the Balinese say – enough water left over even for an ant to drink. Exploited by men, the mountain-born rivers eventually reach the sea.

This is how a popular legend, *Catur Yoga,* describes the invention of rice cultivation on the island: In the beginning, people had only sugar-cane juice to fill their bellies with. Wisnu, the god of water, Lord of the Underground, felt sorry for them, so he came to the surface of the earth to provide men with better food. His methods were brutal, but effective. He raped Earth in order to fertilize her, and she gave birth to rice. Then he made war on the Lord of the Heavens, to persuade him to teach men how rice should be sown, cared for, and harvested. Because the Lord of the Underground won that war, men were taught what they needed to know.

To switch from the juice of sugar-cane to rice, the Balinese had to remake their landscape. The dikes of the ricefields – some low, some

Evening near Besakih. The fan-like crowns of the offerings are fertility symbols, so they will probably be offered to the rice goddess, Dewi Sri.

33

head-high, built of mud or bamboo stakes or wood or stones – run for miles, often in half-circles around the mountain slopes, great flights of stairs descending from the jungle fringes into the valleys below. The people had to build dams on the rivers high up on the hills, and therefore far away from their fields, before the rivers could gather too much force. After building the dams, they had to dig endless conduits, cutting into solid rock and building water tunnels through it. They had to construct wooden, stone, or bamboo-pipe aqueducts to carry the water to the dikes. Another ancient Balinese legend tells of a water conduit being dug along the trail of blood left by a wounded deer. To have made such a journey, that deer must have been endowed with miraculous powers. The Balinese peasants' technique and economic organization showed astonishing complexity and stability.[2] Most of the conduits of Bali's irrigation system lead along slopes and steep mountain ridges, through tunnels some kilometres long, and across aqueducts that span wide and deep gorges. In addition to all that, as the Dutch in the nineteenth century described in detail, and as is still the case, pools had to be excavated for sand deposits and pebbles to prevent clogging of the fields, wooden outlet pipes had to be installed along the length of the conduits to cope with any undue rise in the level of the water, and wooden structures had to be erected at the entrance to every field as a precaution against possible floods. But the most backbreaking part of the job was to keep the system going, to repair the damage caused by repeated floods, landslides, blockages, jungle expansions, monkeys, wild pigs. Only a strong race could keep the land quiet, could retain what had been grabbed from the jungle, always in the

Above: A view of Bali from the southeast, over Gelgel and Klungkung towards the main mountain ridge. This is the place from which most invaders saw Bali first.

Left: One of Bali's still active volcanoes, Batur, surrounded by a lake of the same name.

hope that the volcano above and the sea below would not destroy man's labour in one fell swoop of death.

A strong organization was also required. The *subak* association, whose members own or hold the ricefields, was and still is just such an organization.[3] This is an institution of great importance which is referred to in a royal edict dating as far back as 1022.

The *subak* association wields tremendous power.[4] It decides on the proportion of water to be allocated to each single field owner, and which field should be sacrificed during periods of drought, or other emergencies. It decides when plowing, sowing, or harvesting should begin, who should guard the water in the fields, and who may be excused from work. If a man does not report for his daily chores and is seen 'walking around with a flower in his hair', or if he disobeys the *subak* orders in some other way, the *subak* association will punish him by placing a bamboo pole, with palm leaves bound around it, in the middle of his field, a shamefully visible sign that this man is to be denied the *subak* water, and even the right to work on his field. If he fails to pay the fines which accumulate as a result of his misdemeanors, he may even lose his *sawah* – and this, in times gone by, was often tantamount to economic death. *Subak* rule is harsh, but seldom arbitrary. The *subak*'s highest authority, the *klian*, is rarely described as the holder of his office; it might be more accurate to say that he is 'possessed' by his power, somewhat as a Balinese dancer is possessed by his dance. And *subak* citizens do not simply follow the *klian*'s instructions; rather, they watch his performance, with a scrutiny as penetrating

In spite of the omnipresent threat of Batur, several village communities return after each holocaust, holding stubbornly to their Bali-aga customs. Most beautiful among them, perhaps, is Trunyan, immediately on the shore (overleaf, above left), whose huge banyan tree (below left and overleaf, above right), shadows a very holy temple, Danu Bratan. A god of the netherworld is embodied in a huge statue inside the temple, (overleaf, below right) and it is revered by all the surrounding villages. The Trunyan people have not accepted the Hindu 'innovation' of cremating their dead, but leave them, in old-Balinese fashion, exposed and abandoned at a savagely beautiful cemetery behind a deep ravine in a remote inlet of the lake (overleaf, below left).

as the Balinese audience watching the dance. Every single misstep is noticed. The *klian subak* pronounces verdicts and metes out severe punishments from time to time, but actually he is only applying to a given case the elaborate and detailed rules that are either remembered as customary law or written down in the palm-leaf (*lontar*) constitution of the *subak*. If the *klian* forgets a rule or makes a mistake, a general meeting is called, and a vote is held on the appropriate measures to be taken. Either the constitution is amended, or the *klian* is rebuked and dismissed.

The Balinese ricefields are red when bare, silver and reflect the skies when the water is let in, 'sweet green', as the Balinese say, when the rice is young, golden after it becomes 'pregnant'. The Balinese village, however, is always dark green – shaded by banyan, palm, breadfruit, mango, papaya and banana trees, surrounded – at least in classical times – by brick and mud walls, strangely aloof from the ricefields and the jungle and the world outside. However important the *subak* association may be in the fields in regulating the agriculture of the country, within village limits the *subak* is a minor and marginal force.

The *banjar,* or customary hamlet, was traditionally, and still largely is, the most prominent of the structures ordering the life within the village walls. Like the *subak,* the *banjar* has its own clearly defined membership requirements, its *klian*, and its constitution, which is even more detailed than that of the *subak*, being sometimes several thousand words in length.

Like the *klian subak*, the *klian banjar* can mete out punishment to any *banjar* citizens who infringe upon *banjar* law, and can even condemn the wrongdoers to social ostracism by confiscating their house land and banishing them from the *banjar*. The *klian banjar*, like the *klian subak*, has a great deal of power to help or to destroy, but like the *klian subak*, he too tends to 'follow the public will rather . . . than lead it'.[6]

The Balinese say that the *subak* is held together by 'wet customs' while the *banjar* is based on 'dry customs'. A Balinese qualifies for citizenship in a *subak* if he possesses a ricefield; to be a *banjar* citizen he must possess a hearth. The *banjar* is essentially a settlement unit. Its authorities have jurisdiction over most of the civil matters within the *banjar* limits, such as marriage, divorce, and transfer of property (except rice-land); they were traditionally empowered to keep the village streets clean and safe and the village graveyard sacred. *Subak* citizens may live together as neighbours and members of a *banjar*. But they should always be aware of the distinction between when they must act as *subak* citizens, and when they are governed by *banjar* rules.

It might appear that this is a perfect and clear-cut division of labour; the *subak* orders the common work of the Balinese farmer, while the *banjar* orders the common life of the Balinese villager, and no more is needed. So why do these institutions clash so often and in so many spheres of life? Why are there so many other public organizations, associations, status hierarchies, prestige systems, that contradict, challenge and subvert both *subak* and *banjar* authority, attack one another, each arrogating to itself the exclusive position of being the perfect, the all-embracing, the ultimate order-giving and order-creating institution of Balinese life? Nothing seems to be accomplished in Bali until it is elaborated and complicated to the point where the simple line and original design are entirely obscured.

To complicate matters further, in addition to the structures mentioned above, Bali has been, at least since the days of Majapahit rule, a caste-divided society as well, and again, not in a simple and straightforward way. The castes were largely adopted from Hindu Java – but then they were reinterpreted, recreated, and made to describe a pattern which existed already, in the peculiar Balinese fashion.

> In theory, Balinese theory, all [caste] titles come from the gods. Each has been passed along, not always without alteration, from father to child, like some sacred heirloom, the difference in prestige value of the different titles being an outcome of the varying degree to which the men who have had care of them have observed the spiritual stipulations embodied in them.[6]

The three high castes are Brahmana, Satria and Wesia. From the first of these, *pedandas*, or high priests, always come; the other two castes do not, any longer, in any way correlate with their Indian equivalents.

The three high castes together constitute no more than ten per cent of the population. Yet although the members of these castes are few in number, to themselves, at least, they are of tremendous importance, being descended from the gods. Most people in Bali are Sudras, of the lowest caste – but in Bali, the Sudras are by no means considered to be 'untouchables', and indeed, within this loose classification of Sudra are many subdivisions, some of which constitute 'castes' in themselves, with their own traditions. The *pandé*, or smith's caste, is a case in point – this group has great prestige throughout Bali, and is considered to be magically potent. Like everything else in Bali, caste is, though meticulously and rigidly defined, at the same time fluid. Many Sudras either pretend to be members of the *triwangsa*, or 'three peoples', (three high castes) or they find ways of actually becoming so, through marriage, for instance. Each caste carefully distinguishes itself from the others by such things as posture, particular ways of praying, eating, marriage, house construction, and method of cremation.[7]

Even today, at least in the villages, and among traditional townspeople, when he meets a neighbour who belongs to the *triwangsa*, a Sudra tries to place himself at a lower level if possible, and addresses his neighbour in refined high Balinese, a language of widely differing vocabulary and style from ordinary Balinese.

The twice-born, the Brahmanas, Satrias and Wesias, regard the caste division as the perfect hierarchy along which all of Balinese society should be patterned. They see themselves as superior to the laws of the *subak* and of the *banjar*. Sometimes they even join forces with their equals in neighbouring villages to try to impose their views on the actual working of village politics. The *subak* and *banjar* authorities respect the caste hierarchy and behave strictly in accordance with its rules; they may even regard the caste structure as an ideal, although hardly ever to be attained, model for the Balinese world. And they do everything they can to restrict the higher caste members within the limits of this ideal, to keep nobles from interfering in 'too worldly' matters, particularly in the workings of the *subak* and the *banjar*.

The passion for fighting cocks is common to the people of both mountains and plains. The cocks are objects of tender and unceasing care. They are fed well, and each morning after their obligatory bath are put by the roadside beyond the family compound walls to become hardy and familiar with the noise of people.

Cockfighting is not merely a pastime. The netherworld deities are blood-thirsty and the blood of fighting cocks pleases them most, for fighters are like demons themselves. The cockfight took place at prescribed dates and at magically charged places like crossroads or near the split gate of the temple. Members of the community or associations were obliged to provide a number of cocks commensurate with their importance in community life. Today cockfighting is officially banned.

According to every *subak* and *banjar* constitution, all citizens are absolutely equal in their right to decide public matters. Everybody has one vote in such associations, be he Brahmana or Sudra. Indeed, a majority of the *klians* are – and probably were traditionally – Sudras,[8] and even a man as 'high' as Wesia, for instance, may be a good-for-nothing according to the *banjar* scale of values. Caste in Bali is useful, a Balinese might say, because it shows us how the world should be – and leaves it as it is.

The Balinese are always ready to form associations, *sekahas*, with all kinds of aims, some possible, some impossible. The number of *kulkuls* (alarm drums) still placed in every village square, each for a single association, attests to the almost insatiable fondness of the Balinese for clubs. *Sekahas* are formed for young unmarried men, or for adolescent girls, or for associating people that for a fee do certain jobs, or for mutual aid, or for organizing festivals, or for performing *gamelan* music, or even for old people to drink palm-wine together. *Sekahas* may involve a few people or a large mass; they may last several days or for generations. But each of them has to have special officials, and its own customary or

Above: The ricebin is, in many localities, clearly the major architectural expression of status in the village community, after the ancestor temple. Similarly strict taboos apply to ricebins as to temples, and the bins' pillars and doors are elaborately carved.

Below right: Artefacts, usually symbolizing fertility, are hung on the bins or placed around them.

Above right: Ploughing the ricefields. Often a single compound is built close to the fields outside the village walls to spare selected farmers long journeys to work. Life there is lonely, but also freer from exacting village etiquette.

written law, and each competes with the others in trying to win the exclusive right to run village society and structure village life. It seems that a Balinese can only escape from *sekaha* care when he is at his family hearth. But even there he is not left alone.

A typical Balinese family compound is still (with the exception of those on the 'modern' streets of towns) enclosed by high walls. The only gate is very narrow and is partially blocked by a short wall a few feet inside the yard. Allegedly this is to mislead mischievous demons. But whatever its reason for being, a stranger will not find it easy to intrude into a Balinese house. He is kept away by the very architecture, and also by the internal structure of the place. The family household may appear to be a complete, self-contained, well-protected fortress, secluded from the world. Everything the family needs is inside the enclosure – living quarters, out-houses and barns, three family shrines and also, if only symbolically, the family burial place.

Even a *banjar* official on a special errand who enters the family compound is requested by law to give his message in the politest possible manner and leave quickly. Only a Balinese who respects the family as an institution can even be a member of the *banjar*. A *banjar* citizen is actually a pair, a man plus woman in a common household – father and mother, husband and wife, rarely, unmarried brother and sister or even aunt and nephew. If a family is broken for whatever reason, after a divorce for instance, or the death of a partner, the one who remains alone is usually obliged to leave the *banjar*, because he has become a 'half person'.[9] In some villages, even married but childless adults cannot be citizens of the *banjar*. So it would seem that the Balinese obsession with associations stops at the family gate, that the *sekahas*, and even the *banjar*, respect the family as the ultimate private association. But no wall in Bali is that high, and if we were looking for privacy in our sense of the word, we would have to choose another island.

Families, like *sekahas*, compete with the other segments of the Balinese community, lay claim to be perfect, and expand. They even amalgamate in large patrilineal groups called *dadias*, inbred to a great extent, often highly corporate, engaging in a wide variety of communal activities, questioning, challenging and subverting *banjar* authority, *subak* authority, and the authority of numerous other *sekahas*. Through *dadia* activities in particular, the family sometimes becomes a major source of cultural tension in the village.

In the same way as the *sekaha*, the Balinese family is self-assertive, pushy and vulnerable. Caste cross-cuts the family occasionally, as if there were no walls at all. If a woman, for instance, marries into a higher-caste family, she may be required to use the deferential and self-deprecating language when addressing anybody 'superior' in the family compound, be it even her husband or her own child. Family can resist neither caste nor *sekaha* encroachment if it intends to survive. No family can leave the *subak* if it wants to keep its ricefields. And rarely can a family leave the *banjar*, because for the Balinese outside the *banjar* there is, even today, hardly any life at all.

It is not unusual to see a baby being suckled by any lactating woman within reach. The child is truly 'nursed by the *banjar*' and is obliged throughout his life to address any *banjar* members who are one generation older as 'father' or 'mother', exactly as he addresses his biological parents. In some ways, the *banjar* is as intimate and warm a group as the family, and it is often more important in private life. It is not so difficult, according to the Balinese customary law, to leave one's family. Both the partners can find another spouse inside the *banjar*. But to leave the *banjar* means, for the Balinese, almost the same as 'to lie down and die'.[10]

Neither family nor *banjar, subak* nor caste, is the nucleus of Balinese society, and it often seems to be the basic characteristic of the society that it has no nucleus at all. Balinese society has been compared to an octopus; to a swirl, which turns around an axis that is immaterial and changes at every moment; to a jigsaw puzzle, whose pictures appear according to the way we look at them. Balinese society might also be likened to Balinese dance. Like a Balinese dancer, each segment of society, each *sekaha*, each set of cultural and religious values, moves with extreme concern for its own body, for its own particular existence. And yet for all that, like the dance, *sekaha* existence would be meaningless in its intensive self-absorption if there were no audience – if there were not the Balinese audience, made up of experts *par excellence*, as often as not dancers and performers themselves, watching empathetically the dancing and acting, always ready to correct and challenge. In one typically Balinese dance, the *baris*, (the word means 'military formation'), dancers fight other dancers with long spears, never wounding one another, but fighting fiercely just for the beauty of the fight. In this tumultuous, but at the same time strangely harmonious, dance, the similarity of dancing bodies to the living society seems to be at its closest.

Every Balinese is, from childhood, taught about the possibility of volcanic eruption, about the fragile and perilous frontier between ricefields and

jungle, land and sea, order and anarchy, and he does not need to be taught about the devastation wreaked yearly by monsoons. Every Balinese is trained to remember that his personal happiness and often his very survival depend on how he will respect the frontiers, how well he builds walls around his family and dikes around his fields. There would be no Balinese civilization without these walls. Their simple shape, their elaborate design, their narrow gates allowing only the exact amount of contact between groups of people that is absolutely necessary, or the correct amount of water into the fields, humanize the landscape, and give it form.

> Were there no dividing walls, then the entire village-area would afford nothing to see, other than little clay constructions with grass-roofs, sheltered among coconut palms and fruit trees. These long lines with their countless fine extensions bestow order and harmony on the picture of the *desa*.[11]

Every wall in Bali has its own cultural history. Perhaps the most delicate and fascinating among them is the spiritual wall of detachment and measured intercourse that each Balinese has built around himself.

A feature of the Balinese ethos which has been remarked upon by several Western observers is the 'avoidance of climax', or rather, the lack of the 'sort of climax structure which is characteristic of love and hate in our own culture'.[12] The traditional concept of war and conflict in Bali, for instance, contains 'surprisingly large elements of mutual avoidance'.[13] Vallums and fosses were built (rather like all the other Balinese walls) more in order to keep the distance, to avoid a conflict, than to prepare for war. When two men quarrelled seriously, the authorities used to register their quarrel and order them not to speak to each other, thus attempting not to solve the conflict, but merely to keep the conflicting sides apart. Most verdicts in former times ended in a terrible oath that tended to retain and ritualize the tensions on a level of a steady and non-exploding terror.

The Balinese are aware of the precariousness of their harmony with nature and with one another, and they do everything they can, not to suppress, but to control all that might disturb the balance.

Also, the Balinese notion of personhood is not a suppression of the individual's personality, but a controlling of the precarious tension between the individual and society. All Balinese have personal names, but they are rarely used (outside modern offices and schools). To address one's (socially integrated) elder by his personal name would be considered discourteous. Personal names are 'spoken down' to a person who is too young to be taken seriously, or who is outcast or insane – to anyone who has not been able, for one reason or another, to become a 'complete Balinese'.

> I have asked Rendah for the name of his own mother, who lives in the house with him. He could not remember, and was forced to inquire of the old lady herself. Her husband, Rendah's father, had been dead only six months. He alone of the household had the right to call her by her given name, and if Rendah could not remember it, the old man must not have availed himself of the right for many years.[14]

This does not mean that names are unimportant. The name usually used in addressing a child or a childless person is the birth-order name which denominates a Balinese as the first (Wayan), second (Madé), third (Nyoman) or fourth (Ktut) child of his parents. In addition, kinship terms and

Previous page: A river-crossing near desa Petiga.

44

A hamlet near Sembat. Rice matures. Life in the field is now at its low ebb, as there is not much work to be done while the rice is growing.

Above: One woman raises a flower to her forehead in a gesture of obeisance to a deity; the other flips a petal away. Used blossoms lie on the temple ground.

Right: Flooded sawahs full of plants just after bedding, and sawahs containing mature rice plants. They surround a pond and a shrine for Dewi Danu, the goddess of the lake, who is supposed to take care of the underground tributaries which supply the fields with life-giving water.

teknonymous names ('grandfather of Padma', 'father of Muluk' etc.) are used, as well as names indicating caste, and titles pertaining to office in the village or the *sekaha* hierarchy. Those names distinguish an individual, but they indicate at the same time that a person cannot be identified, or indeed exist in the proper sense, without having some specific standing in society.

One's name is what remains to one when all the other socially much more salient cultural labels attached to one's person are removed. As the virtually religious avoidance of its direct use indicates, a personal names is an intensely private matter. Indeed, toward the end of a man's life, when he is but a step away from being the deity he will become . . . only he. . . may any longer know what in fact it is; when he disappears it disappears with him. In the well-lit world of everyday life, the purely personal part of an individual's cultural definition, . . . is highly muted. And with it are muted the more idiosyncratic, merely biographical, and, consequently, transient aspects of his existence as a human being (what, in our more egoistic framework, we call his 'personality') in favor of some rather more typical, high conventionalized, and, consequently, enduring ones.[15]

As the personality is muted, though not obliterated, so too is time kept under control, insofar as this is possible. The Balinese seem convinced that time, if unbounded – like nature or power or personality – may endanger universal equilibrium and individual balance.

The Balinese have traditionally used two calendrical systems. The first, which is similar to ours, measures the *saka*, or lunar/solar year, and is mostly used for defining the agricultural cycles. The second system, which is perhaps more significant to the Balinese, is the Javanese-Balinese *wuku* system. The *wuku* year consists of 210 days divided into ten different types of weeks, from a one-day week to a ten-day week, all running parallel and simultaneously. Each day of the *wuku* year therefore has ten names, and according to the combination, the day is considered 'full' or 'empty', 'lucky' or 'unlucky'. It is very important that special events should take place on lucky days, and a Balinese, at least until recently, would never, for instance, undertake a journey or transact important business on the wrong kind of day, if he could possibly avoid it.

Obviously, a calendar like this is rather unwieldy for measuring the lapse of time between two sets of dates. And in any case, this is not its purpose. The hours, days and years are identifiable only by their qualities, by their connections to human beings. They do not accumulate in a continuous irreversible sequence, 'they do not build'.[16] The Balinese do not try to immobilize time, any more than they try to stop the rivers from flowing. They merely try to divert the flow before it builds up, accumulates too much strength, and reaches a climax in destructive finality. Time is threatening, in that it is connected with the temporality of man, with aging and death. Thus it is biological time in particular that needs to be controlled with special care.

Every Balinese knows his *oton*, the day, or rather the combination of *wuku* days, on which he was born, and actually feels his fate predestined by the combination. But he rarely counts his *otons*, rarely knows his age – we would even say he is careful not to know it. Balinese life should not be affected by chronological time. The years of life should not quantify in a row with a beginning and an end, and neither should Balinese generations. There is a succession of siblings from the first-born Wayan, to the fourth-born Ktut, but after this one, another 'first-born', another Wayan,

succeeds, identical in status as well as in name with the sibling born three children before him. Similarly, there is a succession of generations from grandson, son and father to grandfather, but then comes the great-grandfather – *kumpi* – in name and status virtually identical with his great-grandson. The great-grandson, as an equal to his great-grandfather, is even forbidden to pay homage to his *kumpi* when the latter dies – a duty absolutely obligatory for everybody else in the community who is junior to the dead man.[17] The oldest and youngest are thus made one, and biological time is made circular.

This is far from being a timeless world, and the Balinese do not try to create such a world. Theirs is a unique human effort to cope with the inexorable passage of time, to soften the sense of the inevitable. The fact of biological aging is countered by the equally real fact of social regenesis.[18] This has nothing to do with nostalgia, and there is nothing for posterity in it. It is a quest by means of which the Balinese try to balance the past and the future, in order to salvage the vulnerable present.

Personality and time are seen as dangerous, and so is space. The Balinese tend to fear any space that has not been organized, touched or quietened by man. The open space is identified with those destructive elements of nature, the sea, the jungles, the volcanoes. Long journeys are still taken in trepidation by villagers. Most Balinese peasants would be upset if they had to sleep alone outside the limits of their family enclosure, or their village. Any wall is welcome to still anxiety.

> . . . the child is impressed with the notion that the world beyond the known cultural area is fraught with a great but undefined danger . . . Like an old hen clucking in panic to call her chicks back under her wings, the mother of the straying child gives a histrionic, fear-laden cry, 'Aroh!', followed by the mention of any one of a dozen scare symbols, chosen at random and without any concern for their relevance. . . . Whenever the child wanders and she wants to recall him, she suddenly exclaims in simulated fear, 'Aroh! Wildcat!' or Aroh! Caterpillar!'[19]

However frightful the cry is, it brings the child close to his mother's comforting lap. *Aroh!* serves to orient him in space, to define that part of space where he is safe. The word *aroh*, metaphorically speaking, is another comforting and reassuring wall.

A person may neglect the warning, he may cross the wall and wander into the open space. But then he exposes himself to becoming *paling* – dazed, dizzy, lost. Then indeed he may bump against a fear that does not propel but stifles him; then he may encounter a fear that is not reassuring but unbearable.[20] Behind the walls there are destructive forces of animalism, of nature, of personality, of time, untamed and unorganized. The walls are fragile and uncertain, and it is only by proper behaviour that each Balinese can keep them standing. Even babies are strongly discouraged from crawling, and if the Balinese want to punish somebody severely, they make him go down on all fours and eat from the pigs' trough. Balance is the main attribute of humanity. A Balinese who does not possess an upright, balanced body is barred from full citizenship. Not only insane or dwarfed persons, but even those lacking a limb, or sometimes even a fingernail, cannot take part in village meetings. It is considered a bad omen not merely physically, but culturally as well, to fall. For instance, a few months ago, in a traffic accident in a village in southern Bali, a woman was wounded; her relatives were trying to carry her home in an upright position, rather than – as would appear to an outsider for the kind

Below: This apparently arduous climb up and down slippery paths is for many a daily routine; people go to the river to bathe, fetch water, and pray.

This girl is Ni Made Suparmiti, soon to be eight years old. 'A man without a child', runs one Balinese song, 'is like a starved buffalo which no tiger would deign to feed on.' A childless woman after death may get an old pig as a companion, and be hunted by it through hell. Children in Bali are expected to be present at childbirth and at a death in the family, and are made to integrate as quickly as possible into the community's network of labour and security. Only babies and very old people can afford to be childish.

of injury she sustained more natural – in a normal, i.e. horizontal, way. A Balinese peasant puts an immense emphasis on the space he lives in being organized and balanced in all its component parts. He calls his village *I Desa* – Mr Village, and describes his household as a human body. The family shrine is the head, the sleeping and living rooms are the arms, the courtyard is the navel, the gate, sexual organs, and the kitchen and granary, legs and feet. The pit in the backyard where the refuse is disposed of is the anus. Almost every Balinese still believes that each part of the body, like each part of the household and the community, possesses a life of its own. The individual is haunted by visions of social disintegration, as he is by the numerous nightmarish graveyard phantoms incarnated some-times in a living leg torn from a body, or in a living trunk without head or limbs. He is made aware that the integrity of the human body, like the integrity of a human community, has to be accepted as vulnerable and has to be protected as a precarious balance of quasi-independent parts that could separate themselves at any moment.

Thus the same metaphor comes to mind again. If Balinese society is like a communal dance, dance can also serve to describe the Balinese ethos. In order to keep the balance, integrity and harmony of a human body and of a social community, it is necessary to put every part of the body and of the community into full play – to allow each of them freedom of express-ion, and freedom to try to control the other parts as much as possible, to compete with them, to contradict and counterbalance them. Only if the *subak* and the *banjar* and the *dadia* and each of the *sekahas,* and individual, and the individual's faculties, are allowed to act fervently to force their own self-centred values and dynamics upon the whole, may balance and continuity in the community and in the individual be assured.

49

THE GODS

Perfumes and scents change into bronze,
a winding sheet turns into gold,
the charcoal then becomes iron,
the ashes are changed to silver,
the fumes are turned into clouds,
the water is becoming rain,
it falls into the human world,
potion of immortality.

The Mantra of Aji Kemban

Perhaps the immensely complicated subject of Balinese religion may best be approached with a warning. 'Better to keep in mind', wrote one of the most distinguished specialists on Bali of our time,[1] 'that under the more or less Hinduized layers of the last ten centuries there is the common Indonesian base, pre-Christian, pre-Muslim and pre-Hindu.'

In describing Balinese religious beliefs and practices, it is much easier not to heed these words. The Balinese themselves call their creed 'Bali-Hindu', and they believe that most of their important gods came from India or Hinduized Java. The gods mostly have Hindu names. There is Trimurti. Surya as the sun god is revered but there is little in him of the Hindu god riding his chariot drawn by seven horses. In Bali, he is rarely personified – there is usually nothing but the name, and an empty throne for him. There is Siwa, the highest god, manifest in almost everything including the highest Balinese mountain, the spirit of the original Balinese ancestor. Uma – Siwa's wife – is believed by the Balinese to be the goddess who delivered their island; and she is also a deity of the Balinese *sawahs*, or wet fields, and *tegalans,* or dry fields. Dewi Sri, the wife of Wisnu, is, as Giriputri, the goddess of Gunung Agung, almost identical in Bali with the Indonesian Mother Rice. As if to make her local flavour even more pronounced, she is sometimes credited with a Balinese daughter, Dewi Melanting, the goddess of seeds and gardens and markets.

There are deities in Bali who not only have a distinctly pre-Hindu, Indonesian or perhaps Polynesian character, but who also still retain their ancient names. There are even some Muslim deities, and a Chinese one, who requires, among his other offerings, 'opium, together with a whole set of opium smoker's equipment'.[2] There is a vast multitude of purely Balinese gods of differing origin, and many of them are known under different names according to the locality or person worshipping them. The gods' mutual relations, their kinship, the stories of their tastes and deeds are immensely rich in detail, and often confusing – that is, typically

Balinese. They are an ornamentation and an embellishment of the beliefs which, beneath the jungle of iconography, are consistent and genuine.

Whatever layers have been superimposed upon it throughout the course of its history, Balinese religion still is – as it was at its obscure beginning – a manifestation of the closeness of the Balinese to their land. When, later, the original nature worship was being developed and refined, it was always in a conscious, incessant, and largely successful effort to explain and humanize the environment. Nature worship grew into a peasant creed, and then it became much more. It matured into a complex religious system that enspirits each community, and the entire country.

Nature worship is still important in Balinese religion. A Balinese praying appears to be enjoying a flower. He holds the bloom between his fingers, dips it into water and then flicks it towards the four winds, for the gods to enjoy too. The fragrance of flowers is supposed to tempt the deities to descend, and an opening flower, a lotus or a banana symbolizes the soul's deliverance, or a sanctuary upon which everything impure can be placed and sent down the river to the all-absorbing sea. The temples are indeed like gardens. Hibiscus, marigolds, dark blue butterfly-pea and frangipanis, blossoms charged with distinctive meanings, some of which bloom in daylight, some at night, grow in a special corner of the temple grounds, ready for the ceremonies. Heavenly nymphs are given flower names, and when they enter the dancers' bodies during a festival, the dancing ladies with their flower-bedecked hair seem like a mass of swaying flowers. When a community prays, the air is heavy with the perfume of flowers. The defeat of a demon is signalled by a flower too – a red hibiscus wilts behind the monster's ear.

In some villages it is forbidden by the Balinese religion to stand a log 'upside down', in a construction, that is to say, in the opposite direction from which it grew.[3] Whenever a tree was cut down, a special prayer accompanied the act, and an offering was laid in the forest temple or shrine of the grove. Old banyan trees were particularly revered, and many of them still contain a little altar in their branches and aerial roots. There are special feasts given in honour of coconut palms, when they are dressed up and flowers are placed all around them. Watching a Balinese carver, one begins to feel that he is praying with his chisels to the spirit of the wood and to the spirit of the stone. Earth is sacred to the Balinese:

> In the Balinese temple it is not the buildings that are essential, but the temple ground. The ground is sacred: on a hallowed plot of land chosen by the gods, the Balinese . . . erect buildings for those gods.[4]

Balinese temples are open, with *balés* and shrines light and elevated on carved pillars and pedestals, as if to embellish the ground and emphasize its sanctity. There are small pavilions and large stones and offering columns in each temple for the guardian of the temple territory and the lord of the soil. There is often a large stone for reverence of the earth, and every temple has a special shrine or a pyramid, or heap of stones at least, for the mountains and their gods. The mountains – and especially Gunung Agung, Great Mountain, the abode of the gods, the peak of Bali – represent the earth in its most holy aspect, grandly elevated.

No ceremony is fully accomplished without a priest consecrating dozens of pots of clear, pure, holy water. Sometimes the Balinese even call their religion *agama tirta*, 'the religion of holy water'. Every spring, every lake, every weir has a temple or a tiny shrine of its own. The water course is the compass of Balinese piety. *Kelod,* which means 'downstream', 'towards the sea', is the direction of darkness, bitterness, the netherworld, while *kaja,* 'towards the mountains', is the direction of light and goodness, the home of the gods. Every temple, every house, every settlement, must be planned along that sacred and dangerous *kelod-kaja* axis. Women during menstruation and sometimes people who have diseases must sleep with their heads in the vile, *kelod* way; anyone else who dared to do so would be risking damnation.

Every morning, a Balinese priest performs a special ceremony for the sun. Every pious Balinese housewife makes offerings to the sun three times a day. In the elevated *kaja*/east corner of every temple in Bali, and of every household, there is an empty throne, *padmasana,* sometimes lavishly carved in stone, sometimes simply built of split bamboo, but always the artistic masterpiece of the place. The throne, lovingly adorned, waits for the sun to descend to meet the human beings. The sun, the most powerful force in nature, is the highest and most divine of the Balinese gods.

The Balinese invoke the spirit of nature, appealing to the gods to enter stones of striking shapes, flowers, dancing girls and the wafting smoke of incense. But they rarely let water choose its natural course, and they worship nature in order to change it – as only devoted peasants do.

Rice, the most revered of all the holy flowers and plants, became truly a god in Bali. The pious Balinese reaps the first stalks in silence. The rice should be handled only in the daytime. When it is served, on some ceremonial occasions, it should be set on a pedestal higher than the person eating, and there are rules prohibiting speech with a man eating rice lest it anger the spirit that is entering him. A mark made of rice is painted onto the foreheads of those who have said their prayers. Rice represents a vital power at many ceremonies. And sheaves of rice buried in a new dam are a plea to the gods to make the structure sound.

There is a close connection in Bali between all sacred matters and rice. The temple is, after all, the agricultural beginning of a settlement, the first stretch of land seized from the jungle, the victory, demonstrated by a piece of cleared ground. The gods in Bali were 'the first settlers', the ancestors who first came and 'asked for rice'.[5] The rulers of the village are wardens of the soil, but the gods are the owners of the soil. Water is holy because it is precious and because it is essential for making sense of the cleared ground, turning it into *sawahs,* fields where rice can grow. There is hardly a single temple in Bali that is not to some extent and in some aspect a fertility temple too.

Before any work begins in the terraced ricefields, called by the Balinese 'the steps of the gods', the representatives of each irrigation association – *klian subak,* priests and selected citizens – still today travel upstream, in the *kaja* direction, towards a weir or spring or lake. There they propose the requisite offerings (in former times they threw gold into the lake), and invite the water deity to descend and visit the *subak* temple. This is the Water-Opening Ceremony, which takes place at different times in different communities. Only after the deity is satisfied and gives consent can water be brought from the holy source and used to purify the land downstream. Another ceremony has to be held to clean the irrigation system. A suckling pig, a white duck and a chicken, and sometimes some other offerings, are sacrificed at the point where the water is to be diverted from the main conduit into the secondary ones leading towards the *sawahs* below. Only after all this has been done may the first rice sprouts be planted, even then in a strictly prescribed ritual manner.

Above: a huge banyan tree looms over Pura Kehen, the former monarchical temple of the princedom of Bangli.

Opposite, above: Pura Ulun Siwi (see page 22) during the Galungan festival.

Opposite, below: Merus in the inner court of Pura Taman Ayun in Mengwi. Merus symbolize the universe – their lowest part, of stone, is the netherworld; the middle, the transient world, is usually wood; the roofs of bamboo tiles and palm fibres are heavens.

For about three months after planting, ceremonial life is rather subdued and so is the tenor of the peasants' daily routine. Nevertheless, hardly a week passes without a ritual service or offering being made: the gods are present and waiting for the grain to make its appearance, for the 'pregnancy' of the rice to be definitely assured. Now comes the time when the rice is treated like a woman with child, spoken of tenderly, affectionately satisfied in 'her longing for sour food, spices and sweets', and of course flowers are presented to 'her' in abundance. This is a happy time. Expectation and the rhythmic pulse of the rituals gain in intensity, ever more elaborate offerings are made, the rice turns golden, water is drained from the fields, and everybody prepares for the glorious harvest.

Either three or five days prior to the beginning of the harvesting a few of the best rice stalks are cut. One leaf is left on each stem. The bunches of stalks are bound together, forming *ninis*, each *nini*, or 'rice mother' being entered by the divinity of Dewi Sri. . . . When the sheaves have been stacked in the storage sheds, a *nini* is placed on top of the sheaves to spread her blessing over the rice. Just before the rice supply is finished, the stalks forming the *nini* are also threshed, and a portion of the grain is then placed in each of the sleeping apartments of the family to bring good luck and the certainty of many descendants. The chaff and straw are scattered . . . as an offering to the water deities.[6]

Small flower and food offerings are placed on each terrace of the *sawah* fields by farmers on days specifically prescribed by the Balinese calendar. There are small stone altars, *beduguls*, near each important water divider, worshipped by a 'water team', and there is a fully elaborate temple at the dam or above the highest of the fields where the whole *subak* meets once an agricultural year.

If the gods were neglected in Bali, as a priest warns in one of his prayers, famine would play havoc with the land, pestilence would attack the villages, crops would fail, beasts die, the earth tremble and quake, and rivers would flood their banks. Nothing can ever be more important to the Balinese than serving their gods, and everything has to take second place when the gods so demand. But should the water happen to run the wrong way, if the soil or rice should desire it to be otherwise – then without much ado a temple standing in their way is torn down, the temple ground is turned into a *sawah* or water conduit, or is flooded by a dam. The gods have no choice but to yield to the needs of the crops.

Balinese religion appears as a harmonious, beautifully syncopated sequence of rites, ceremonies and festivals. But when watched more closely, it also appears to be a mechanism, a timetable for the co-ordination of ploughing and planting, replanting and harvesting, harmonization of the cycles of each sawah terrace and dam, inside a *subak*, and the whole valley. The Balinese temples and shrines are a charming and refined addition to the Balinese landscape; they are also an elaborate and dynamic mapping of the valley's agricultural network, marking the crucial points of water dislocation, soil limits, climate factors, imprinting them on the mind of every Balinese and into the Balinese cultural matrix.

Only once in a season is there the right amount of water available at a given place in a Balinese valley. The religion, the busy ritual calendar, the demanding, exacting offerings, the endless prayers, the beating of the right signal drum at the right temple gate and at the right moment – all these acts of piety also ensure that each community, each purified and blessed plot of land, gets the proper attention, is ploughed, watered, planted and harvested so as to yield the best possible crop. The Balinese religion may

Above: The main gate of Pura Kehen.

Right: The same gate seen from the kaja direction. The Kehen temple is mentioned as early as AD 1204, in an edict prescribing the types of festivals appropriate for the temple and villages around.

appear baroquely over-ornamented to an uninitiated observer, but for the Balinese peasants it was, and still is, the 'science of the holy water', a 'ritual store of information'[7] complicated only to the degree that Balinese agriculture requires it to be.

Some students of Bali consider neither nature worship nor the peasant agricultural creed but rather the cult of the ancestors to be the most important element of Balinese religion.[8] The Balinese religious practices are often said to be principally efforts to renew and maintain a contact with the departed forefathers; Siwa is invoked as 'grandfather' by the Balinese peasants, and so are the deified Balinese kings. The cult of the ancestors is not merely another face of Balinese religion. It is rather a method of uniting the worship of nature and the peasant creed so that they come to have a spirit of belonging to one womb, a spirit of communal solidarity at a family level, a village level, and throughout the whole island.

In classical times, each social group, from family to kingdom, was also a temple congregation, and there is still virtually no recognized social group in the island that has not its own temple or complex of shrines. Each Balinese, in order to remain a respectable citizen, has to pray in several temples and to participate in several temple congregations, as there is not any other way through which he can validate his standing as a member of a family, caste, village, or irrigation association. This, at least, was the case in classical times, and is still largely true at present, for most of the peasant population at any rate.

From the countless tiny *sanggahs kemulan*, or shrines of origin, that are in all traditional households, prayers are addressed to family ancestors, family gods, and to the ancestors and gods of the *banjar*, village, province and island (or kingdom, when kingdoms still existed). The same nature gods, the same peasant gods, the same ancestors are revered throughout the island. Because of that there is still a spiritual link which unites every temple of the country with every other, from literally the smallest holy

In an ancient Balinese romance, there are seven seas which the hero has to cross to find a princess or to calm his soul – the watery sea, the salt sea, the sea of honey, the sea of mud, the sea of sand, the sea of blood and the sea of fire. There is only one kind of sea around Bali, but it appears to the Balinese to contain all the horrors any fable could invent. The sea is dangerous and must be appeased with continual offerings.

Above: At the black-sand beach near the demon temple at Tegal Tamu, a pemangku and his female assistant seem alone to confront the sea – but in fact the beach behind them is full of people watching, praying, waiting for the blessing.

Right: Tanah Lot, a sea temple on Tabanan coast adorned for the festival but empty except for a priest who is preparing the shrines for the next day. This is one of the temples accessible only at low tide.

stone to the magnificent Pura Besakih. If there is anything which can be called fundamental to the Balinese religion, this is it; precisely because the religion was founded upon and remained nature worship, peasant creed and cult of the ancestors, it could survive among the pragmatic Balinese to this day.

There are several kinds of priests in Bali, each with his own (if not always clearly defined) function and field of authority. *Balians usada*, medicine-men, are consulted when a person is in trouble or sick, to find out whom a child is an incarnation of, to find a stolen article or a thief, and are some-times called upon to inaugurate a new building. *Dalangs,* puppeteers of the shadow play, grace tooth-filings, weddings, or births which have taken place at a wrong conjunction; *dukuhs*, originally perhaps, as their name suggests, hermits, formerly influential in many fields, are now restricted to the district of Karangasem, and almost forgotten elsewhere.

By far the most important priests in their day-to-day function are the *pemangkus*, who number at least 20,000 in a population of not much more than two million. The *pemangku* serves as the priest of the congregation, the guardian of the temple, and he is the most active and most visible officiant at the Balinese festivals. He is truly the priest of the people.

Pedanda and *sungguhu* priests are much less numerous (there are several hundred *pedandas* now, and still fewer *sungguhus*). They might appear as strangers amidst the Balinese crowd, praying in their own self-absorbed way. Yet through their action and interaction, the dynamics and the

essence of the Balinese religion can perhaps best be seen.

The *pedanda* is the high priest, a member of the highest Brahmana caste. It is said that he mostly understands the Sanskrit he uses in his prayers. He believes in merging with the Supreme Void and in achieving 'thirstlessness' through meditation. The *sungguhu*, according to legend, was originally a high priest too, but was later demoted for faulty, or shocking, behaviour, so he is now a Sudra.[10] While the *pedanda* serves the gods, the *sungguhu* is the priest for the world of the demons.

The *pedanda* and the *sungguhu* are equally distinguished and proud (the *sungguhus*, because they are less numerous, are even more costly to order for ceremonial occasions). Both are clothed in white robes, and both tie their hair in a similar priestly knot, but the *pedanda*'s is on the top of his head, while the *sungguhu*'s is on his neck. Both sprinkle holy water and scatter flowers during the ceremony, except that the *pedanda* uses an upward movement, and the *sungguhu* flings his flowers in the direction of the earth. Both perform similar *mudras* with their hands, both intone similar *mantras*, except that the *pedanda*'s prayers are accompanied by an angelic tinkling of a prayer bell, while those of the *sungguhu* are accompanied by the deafening noise of the conch shell, chiming bells, and a double drum manipulated by one or more of the *sungguhu*'s assistants.

The offerings which are consecrated by the *pedanda* and *sungguhu* contain ingredients that are very much alike – only the rice in the *sungguhu*'s offerings (*caru*) is more spicy, the meat raw, the flowers wilted (or sometimes made from entrails), and there is more palm wine and alcoholic spirit. The smell is pungent, as the incense used is often made from dung. The offerings of the *pedanda* are beautifully elaborate, and laid upon high pedestals – for Siwa still higher than for the other gods. The *sungguhu*'s offerings appear messy to divine or refined human eyes, and are placed on the ground where the demons – and the dogs, the demons' usual embodiment – can satisfy their devilish hunger and monstrous thirst.

In every Balinese temple, at any religiously important spot in the courtyard, at the crossroads, in the fields, at the gate, leaf-trays with portions of every meal are placed, incense is burned, flowers are spread. As neither gods nor demons ever seem to be satisfied, the ritual offering has to be repeated every few hours, every few days, and sometimes on a large and even monumental scale when a yearly, decennial or even centennial ceremony is performed, involving the whole community, or even the entire island. Time is filled by the complicated religious calendar. Propitiating the demons is as continuous a flow of activity in Bali as propitiating the gods.

The customary festivals in the *wuku* year are held, as a rule, on the anniversaries or *odalans* of the individual village temples. There are often more than fifteen of them, but we have to add to this number tens or even hundreds of *odalans* celebrated in a village's family temples as well as at supravillage sanctuaries, including the temples of the state.

The Balinese religious calendar may appear confusing to an outsider, and even in Bali only expert priests are able to control and direct the whole affair. What an ordinary Balinese is supposed to understand, however, is just the endless continuity of the ritual, and its essence, which is manifest in each single one of those countless events.

A priestess praying to the deity of a holy-water spring. Incense, fanned by the dance-like movement of the hand, is an indispensable vehicle for carrying the essence of the offerings to the gods.

59

Perhaps the most holy and most revealing among the Balinese festivals are those marking the culmination of the *wuku* and *saka* years – the great ceremonies of Galungan and Nyepi. Galungan is a huge and beautiful annual (210 day) festival, celebrating the deified forefathers who are descending to earth for a short visit. The ancient *Usana Bali* mentions that the days before Galungan are dangerous rather than pleasing, because before the ancestors come, the *kalas* and *butas* arrive from the netherworld abode, and their aim is to harm mankind. This is still the case. The ominous days are lived through, fully spent in preparing the great feast for the divine guests. Thus, apparently, through work and devotion, the threat from the netherworld guests is countered. The celestial visitors then come, stay for five days or so, are entertained by their heirs, and after they safely depart again an exuberant celebration is held by the people and a new wave of ceremonies takes place, reaching its zenith at Kuningan, ten days after Galungan. It is made clear by the priests and all the pious Balinese throughout those days that the offerings are made to the demons, the *kalas* and *butas*, as well as to the gods and the deified ancestors – to keep the balance between the divine and chthonic during those days is what matters most.

During Nyepi, the solar New Year, even more than at Galungan, the accent is on the dangerous 'time before'. On the day preceding Nyepi, on the last night, 'sleeping moon', of the ninth Kasanga month, at the spring equinox, the houseyards, many temples' grounds, and the crossroads are virtually covered with *caru* offerings, lights burn the whole night, cockfights are held in every village. Drums and bells are beaten, conch shells blown, during this largest ceremony for the netherworld. But an altar is inevitably also erected for the highest celestial deity – the god of the sun. Nyepi, the next day, is the time of silence. Suddenly no prayer is said, no candle lit, no work done, love-making is forbidden, everybody just waits for the next morning, when balance will be restored. With that sunrise, as a *pedanda* explained, 'the world comes', the gods may bathe again, girls are allowed to wash their hair at the springs and ask the priest for holy water, blessed rice, and fire to light the family hearth anew.

There are many local variations to these ceremonies, but everywhere in Bali it is only through the dramatic and ostensibly precariously engineered spectacles of Galungan and Nyepi that the Balinese can usher in the ancestors and the new year, and with them a new round of priestly prayers. Pleasing the demons and pleasing the gods are for the Balinese equally important activities, and, in a strangely touching way, they seem to be equally reassuring.

Whatever the calendrical occasion, it is always considered fitting for Rangda and Barong to show up, and their fight, when it comes to that, always constitutes the high point of the ceremony. It is so, perhaps, because in their drama the dynamics and meaning of the Balinese religion are made even more explicit than elsewhere.

Rangda we have already met briefly in another role – as Mahendradatta, conquering Javanese princess of early Balinese history. But Rangda is, first and foremost, the queen of the Balinese netherworld, the horrible sister of Kala, the more awesome face of Durga – undoubtedly the most evil of the Balinese demons. Whoever sees her appearing at dawn, often

Gate of the pura balé agung of desa Sempidi (above), and (below), detail of the split gate of a temple in Sangsit.

Right: The wife of a pemangku who is so highly esteemed that when her husband died the villagers insisted she take his place as pemangku.

Above: The Barong Landung, revered as deities, return from their symbolic bath. The black giant is Jero Gedé, the Big One, and his companion is Jero Luh, the Female. These are very holy and powerful figures, and the erotic content of the folk songs which accompany their appearance suggests that they were originally connected with fertility rites.

Previous page: Shortly before sunset people bathe. Also, magically charged objects like ancient weapons and masks are taken to the seashore or riverside to be purified. This is a purification of masks at a temple of holy springs near Sangsit.

after a night-long ceremony spent invoking her, can never forget her figure towering against the temple gate, her necklace of human entrails, her huge breasts swinging as she dances, her exposed sexual organs, her hot aggressiveness, her claws, her tusks, her urge to kill, her laugh, her eyes. Rangda, almost always danced by a man, can play and dance alone or in *Calonarang,* as a witch fighting a king or king's minister because the king (or his son in another version) rejected Rangda's daughter. But the drama is most complete and religiously revealing if the Barong appears as Rangda's counterpart and enemy.

There are Barongs representing pigs, tigers, lions, wild boars, elephants, cows, deer, horses, dogs, goats, quails and even caterpillars, but their appearance is not too impressive, and their roles are largely comical or marginal. Barong *keket* (or *rentet*) is, however, '*the* Barong'. Not comparable to any known animal, yet having something of many of them, he is huge and splendid. Played by two male dancers, the first in the front, the second inside the hind legs, the Barong often fills the whole court of a small temple. When not in action, he resides in a special fenced-in *balé* in a temple, tended by those who reverently call him Banaspati Raja, or Lord of the Jungle.

The Barong generally appears before Rangda does. He circles the village, then the area in front of the temple gate (usually), sometimes spreads a mat for distinguished citizens, dances for the villagers, and waits. When Rangda appears, it is like lightning. They rush at each other, fighting furiously. Eventually, more often than not, Rangda succeeds in stuffing her magic weapon, a piece of white cloth, *anteng,* into the Barong's mouth. Shouting horribly, exultant, she prepares for a dance of victory. It never comes to that, however. The village men and women join in the fight, attacking Rangda. Barong, now recovered, fights along with them but the witch, laughing and shouting with bloodcurdling yells, waves the same puissant white cloth above their heads; this seems to make them all go quite mad, and they turn their weapons against their own bodies. This is *ngurek,* and would be the climax of the ceremony, if climax played any part in Balinese culture. Nothing ends, in fact. Rangda is eternal; Barong is never defeated; the villagers are not harmed by their own violent self-stabbing, since they have been made invulnerable by the Barong. All retire from the scene, their fight indecisive, and all know the drama will be re-enacted time and again.

The outsider must not be tempted to interpret the fight as being simply one of good against evil. The very appearance of the Barong is ambiguous, and in any case far from being simply godlike.

> The Barong as a personality was at once awesome and loveable. He had the attraction of a pet animal with endearing, capricious ways and a charm of his own. One could not help being fond of him when he would run about, fuss his head, wiggle his behind, and tinkle the little bell on his tail. He was as gaily decorated as a toy, his fluffy coat invited an affectionate pat. He would wear flowers in his silken beard. Even though his great eyes bulged and his teeth snapped fearsomely, he was a lovely being.[11]

When the Barong circles a village, it is believed he makes it safe against witches. His hair protects children from nightmares, and the most powerful among Barongs can even consecrate holy water. Barong is perhaps derived from a pre-Hindu protective animal, 'friend of the ancestor'; or he may be connected with ancient Tantric Buddhism, or early Wisnuism.

In any case, Barong is clearly part of the *kelod,* netherworldly, sphere of

Left: The Pura Dalem of Kesiman on festival eve. Once a year, about three weeks after Galungan, Barongs from temples near and far are brought here to be revitalized by the holiness of the place.

Below: The most holy kaja/east corner of the demon temple in desa Tegal Tamu. To enter the temple, one has to pass through a maze of the aerial roots of a banyan tree, which makes a canopy, itself part of the weird architecture of the place.

the Balinese universe. Indeed, Barong is also called 'the Lord of the Graveyards' by the Balinese. His magic is 'white' against the 'black' magic of Rangda, but his attendants, like those of Rangda, are horrifying spooks and phantoms. Barong guards people against Rangda – but he is a demon too.

As Barong is not merely good and benevolent, so Rangda does not merely delight in evil and annihilation. Rangda, to an unbeliever, seems a brutal offence to a sense of beauty. But why do the Balinese, frightened and fascinated by her, often play the *gamelan legong* for her, the finest, most tender and intricate music they are able to produce? Rangda dances to inspire fear, she shouts of her hunger for corpses and her thirst for blood – but her eyes betray her. Her long claws are visibly trembling, she is helpless in her violence. She, too, is afraid!

Rangda's terrible weapon, the *anteng*, the thin white cloth that strikes men down and makes the Barong bite the dust, is the same as the *anteng* by which every Balinese mother carries her baby when it is still too small to walk. Rangda is horrible. But it is Rangda who is called upon by the Balinese in times of unbearable distress. A western observer noted, 'Rangda, appearing very detached and "innocent", dances near to [a man

attacking her with a *kris*] as if drawn there, holding her cloth partly folded and like a child in her arms.'[12] The bearing of many children is considered to be a boon in Bali that only chthonic deities can confer, and Rangda is also associated with the fertility principle.[13] The devils living underground in Bali threaten life, but they also keep the seeds of flowers, trees and rice, and the seed of men, too. The netherworld is close to the graveyard, and smells of death. But at the same time it is the place where new life germinates.

Rangda is nakedly and excitingly a woman. Some Balinese even describe the Barong's attack on her as an attempt at rape. Both Rangda and Barong come from the dark. They stand in eternal opposition, and are as close as woman and man can be to each other. Since time immemorial a violent struggle has been waged between these two great figures, and still the Balinese watch the drama breathlessly, in awe and adoration – for its epic power, but surely also for its message that death is intimately close and life is always about to emerge out of its shadow.

According to some pundits, the abode of the gods and also the abode of the demons is represented in every human body: the netherworld and the demons' *pura dalem* temple by the mouth, throat and the crown of the head; heaven and the celestial *pura puseh* temple by the top of the head – a spot which will open with due meditation; the world of human beings and the community central temple, called most often *pura desa,* or *pura balé agung,* by the forehead, exactly between the eyebrows. Those three centres in the body, and those three corresponding temples, one pundit said, 'control the magical energy, *sakti,* which flows through mankind'.[14]

The Balinese believe that the gods reside on high, on or above the mountains. The celestial *pura puseh* temple, therefore, the temporary abode of the gods when they come to visit the human beings, has to be on the *kaja,* towards the mountains, outskirt of a settlement. *Pura puseh* means literally 'navel temple'. Celestial deities are worshipped here, which in Bali means also, or primarily, the original ancestors, those who began the community's life.

On the opposite side of the settlement, in the *kelod,* devilish, direction, sometimes actually by the sea and submerged by the high tide, is the *pura dalem,* the demon temple. The temple is often intimately connected with the graveyard, and there is always a mournful *kepuh* tree nearby. Devils, vampires, monsters and spooks watch and judge every step; or just a glaring, threatening eye, carved in stone or merely imagined, may be the watcher. The *pura dalem* is eerie and frightful, the *pura puseh* lovely and light, but both are essential. There has never been a community in classical Bali which did not have both the celestial and the chthonic temple, both equally cared for, each the object of deeply felt and beautifully expressed affection.

On the axis connecting the celestial *pura puseh* temple and the demon temple, *pura dalem,* the third main community temple is located, the *pura balé agung,* the temple 'of the large hall' or of the great council. The temple is culturally as well as topographically central, and is often the most elaborate and richly decorated. Here the rites for the founders of the social order are held. This is the true temple of *madyapada,* the in-between world; that is also *mertyapada,* the world of human beings.

The *pura balé agung* symbolizes all the Balinese nature, peasant and ancestor beliefs; it is the Balinese religion expressed in its nucleus. The highest, *kaja,* court of this temple is devoted to the worship of the celestial gods. Opposite stands the lowest, outer, or *kelod,* court, where the netherworld cult is located. And in between, there is the *balé agung,* 'the essential

building in the essential court',[15] a large assembly hall where the community council meets to pray and to govern.

The *balé agung* lies in the magically charged centre between the infernal and celestial spheres and is permeated by both.[16] The oldest members of the community, those who are descended directly from the founders of the settlement and the officials of the village, are considered closest to the ancestors and gods and in some villages still are seated at the *kaja* end of the hall. In these localities, the *kelod* part of the *balé agung* is reserved for members of the community who are not yet fully accepted, alongside those degraded for some reason, and those charged with the care of the village streets, the cockfight ring and graveyard. Those villagers are marked by their contact with evil, and through them the netherworld is permitted to enter the hall and speak out at the meetings.

A session in the *balé agung*, therefore, could never be just a village assembly. Whenever the council meets, it is a meeting of men, gods and demons to deliberate together, share a sacred meal, and act out a ceremony of the civic religion; it is sometimes a momentous and sacred occasion when the clash between the forces of *kaja* and the forces of *kelod* builds up to a crescendo – and it is the men who are expected to control the clash.

The Balinese are never allowed to forget their gods and demons. To be Balinese has always meant to be involved in continuous religious activities. No one is ever spared. The temple congregation, *pemaksan*, means, literally, 'obligatory work'. To believe in the religion of Bali is a heavy burden, shockingly expensive. Often the time consumed by the preparations of offerings alone 'probably approaches that consumed by manual labor once terracing has been completed'.[17] It goes on day after day, hour after hour. Hundreds and often thousands of multicoloured and multiform offerings have to be made to attract the deities to the temple. And it is of basic significance that all the religious duties have to be performed in groups and equally distributed throughout the community.

When the time of festival comes, the whole community gathers. The shrines are clothed, pendants made of palm leaves on long bamboo poles are erected everywhere, and demons of stone at the temple gate have a flower tucked behind their ears. The temple is now like a village common on market day – only busier, noisier, happier, and more colourful. Balinese ceremonies are not the place for inward contemplation or private prayer. It is a time of bustle and warmth, *ramé*, and *ramé* in itself is seen as a wonderful condition of being, a guarantee of safety.[18]

The Balinese are happy and relaxed when they are together, closely packed into a temple court that often seems too small to hold them all. They appear certain that even the most powerful deities and monsters will not be able to resist their festivities, and that all of them, attracted by the music, the colourful offerings, and the joyful atmosphere, will join in the prayer and dance, and in so doing, be truly involved in community life.

The Balinese cosmos is a tumultuous one. Each person is constantly reminded of the perils of his daily existence on the razor-edge bridge between *kaja* and *kelod*, gods and demons, heaven and hell, in the midst of their eternal warring that threatens at any moment to annihilate him and his island. Hardly any other religion has created a universe with such a fragile centre as that of the Balinese. But the islanders appear to know the remedy. Everyone, if pious enough, can multiply his strength through *ramé*, and through identifying himself with many wealthy and sound communities. Also, if he worships the gods and demons devotedly enough, his soul may become immortal, and he himself may become a *protégé* brother of the giants, as powerful as any pundit can imagine.

Above: In the temple court after the procession, holy water and flowers are distributed. Some of the water is drunk, the remainder sprinkled on the hair and body.

Opposite. All offerings must contain fire (incense), water and flowers. Of course, rice, the basic food of the Balinese, is almost never missing. Some offerings have all their components, structure, shape and colour-combinations minutely prescribed. Others show a more individual inventiveness and beauty. The offerings are usually made by women.

A newborn baby, today as in the fifteenth century, is welcomed ceremoniously, and addressed in highly polished language as *jeroné*, 'your highness'. The utterances of the baby are received as holy messages from the other world. If the baby happens to die before losing its first teeth, its 'way back' is short and easy, if there is a journey at all. The dead baby need not be purified by any of the numerous prescribed death rituals, because it is still pure – it can be buried without delay, and in the most *kaja*, most elevated corner of the village cemetery.

When the child is 105 days old (in some places a different age may be prescribed), the mother is allowed to let her baby's feet touch the ground gently for the first time, and a worldly name is given to the child. Yet the 'descent' to the world of human beings takes a good deal longer. Virgin boys and girls, 'flower youths', are still considered, in some old-fashioned villages, purer than most of the respected adults in the community, and are entrusted with certain solemn tasks in serving the gods. Only after marriage does a traditional Balinese merge completely with the profane. He becomes a full citizen, his views are heard at the *desa*, *banjar* or *subak* councils, he matures as a personality. This is the period of life when he is most human, and farthest from the gods.

Virtually no rites of passage are reserved for a Balinese during this, the longest, stage of his life. All he can do is wait and see that the rites for his children and for his dead are properly performed. He grows older, moves higher in worldly hierarchies, works, becomes tired and weak, until gradually he leaves the councils one by one and approaches his death – which is at the same time his glorious homecoming. He 'turns little again' and is addressed in polished language, just as he was when he was a baby. Even if his speech degenerates into senile mumbling, it should be accepted as a pertinent message from the other world. The past is forgotten, and the future is being remembered. The human and mortal personality evaporates, but not the respect the old person enjoys in his community. He is revered now, because he is drawing close again to the realm beyond, the only place where a new birth, a new life may germinate again.

> *What is in the beginning? It is death. What follows then?*
> *He is ash.*
> *Of what use are waters, land and other . . .*
> *Of what use is the power to create crawling and coiling*
> *serpents and tigers,*
> *While one does not overcome death?*
>
> Jnanasiddhanta

A term for 'to die' in Balinese also means 'to go home'. The dead body is washed, then water, earth and flames purify the body, reduce it to ash. When, finally, after many complicated and repetitious ceremonies, the dead body is destroyed, the purified and deified soul closes the circle for a while. The end merges into the beginning, the death into life, the spirit of the dead, the ancestor, the god (through a villager in trance) can speak in a babyish voice, can address the pious community as 'mamas' and 'papas' and can be spoiled and indulged (the term *sayangang* means to 'indulge' a child, as well as to 'worship' a god) by his descendants who now pray to him.

There is no popular belief in ultimate salvation (only high priests want to reach the state of thirstlessness). There is nothing in the passage through life and death to interrupt the circle of eternity. The most desired blessing that can be bestowed upon an ordinary person is that he become a soul so purified, an ancestor so deified, as to be privileged after four generations

One explanation of the term for the Brahmana priest, 'pedanda', is that he is a staff-bearer, his staff, 'danda', being like the Hindu gods' ceremonial weapons. The staff is often topped by a crystal ball, 'the glitter of the sun'. It ends in four inturned darts around a central straight dart, like the vajra, thunderbolt of Indra.

have passed to return to earth – some Balinese say as dew, others say as love, to enter the household of blood-relatives again, to close the circle for a while, enspirit another Balinese baby.

Whenever a Balinese is born, four elder brothers, *kanda mpat* (or sisters, if the baby is a girl), emerge from the womb with the infant. They manifest themselves in the amniotic fluid, the blood, the vernix caseosa and the afterbirth; they originate both in heaven and hell, are both demonic and divine, and stay around throughout one's life and on beyond. When neglected, they cause all sorts of pain during a lifetime, and after death they punish the wicked soul. When properly revered (the first drop of milk should be theirs, the last thought of the day, and much more too) they keep watch day and night, and can be summoned by name when protection is needed. The legend of the four brothers is a charged subject in the Balinese religion, and it is rather difficult for a foreigner to get a Balinese to speak about it.

Also, there are many variations on the legend.[19] According to one of the more common versions, Angapati, born as amniotic fluid, lives in the underbelly of man, protects the sacrum in times of danger, enables him to hear, and also rules every kind of shrine and is the lord of animals. Mrajapati, the birth blood, resides in the liver, allows man's blood to flow, and is also the master of mountains and forests, and governs any journey from one place to another. Banaspati, the natal cord, resides in the bile, guards the flesh, and also rules over the soil, cultivated or barren. Banaspati Raja, the afterbirth and the strongest of the four, moves into the kidneys, binds the veins and arteries together, and at the same time is lord of the graveyards, streams and brooks, and the spirit of the glorious Barong, who fights Rangda and defends Bali against her claws.

The *kanda mpat* are immensely powerful giants – according to some priests, the most powerful giants of all. They move the Balinese cosmos – but it is always up to the individual to decide when their forces are devilish, when benevolent, and when they are merely being held in reserve. It is scarcely possible to imagine the enormity of the *kanda mpat*, yet they are the brothers of each Balinese, born of the same mother, into the same courtyard. They are boundless – yet wholly contained in the tiniest drop of a person's blood, semen and sweat.

Many things in Bali disappeared without a trace after the *puputans* of 1906–8, others have more gradually disappeared. But the essentials of the religion still hold fast. The Balinese who prays and believes is still both proud and afraid – conscious of standing in the centre of the universe, where divine and demonic powers meet, conscious of the ominous and elevating truth, that his duty and his fate is to keep the struggle within limits.

The pious Balinese works hard to release the powers of the netherworld and heaven, and to channel them for the well-being of the community. He invokes the calamity and then wanders through the danger, praying, dancing, being with his neighbours and his kin; through the sharing of religious duties, he splits his fear.

The most powerful of the kanda mpat, the four brothers/sisters one is born with in Bali, is said to be manifest in a most delicate fluid within the body, assuring the fineness of form and delicacy of balance which is identical with the source of vitality and the power to breathe. This girl, like hundreds of others, walked in a long procession for more than ten kilometres, bearing the fresh flowers of her headdress as if they were gold, and bearing the gold as if it were fresh flowers.

Above: As cremation is very expensive, the poorer Balinese often share their more prosperous consociate's ritual, and partake of its splendour. On this occasion, about forty cremations took place.

Above right: Arca lingga or pratima (figures made of gold, precious wood, or, as here, old coins sewn together) are kept in a temple until, at the temple festival, deities are invited to enter the figures and make them alive. North Bali, c. 1800.

Right: Offerings are placed in front of a cremation coffin.

Far right: The back of a cremation tower, in which the body is carried from family compound to cremation field.

Below left: A puppet of Hanuman, monkey hero of the 'Ramayana' from a cremation. When two performances are staged, one is in the daytime, therefore without shadows, and hence without a screen. This is strictly for an invisible audience 'of gods and souls only'.

Below centre: A cremation coffin on fire.

Below: Immediately after, before the white bone-ash is separated from the wood-ash and taken to the sea, or kept for other rites of purification.

THE RULERS

To the Balinese this dance, which to us seems so dramatic, is merely a bodily display. The Baris dancer threatens or cowers before no imagined foe; he only tests the power of his wide-opened eyes. He reads no oracle on his outspread fingers, he only admires his hands; and when he seems to scan the horizon he is only displaying another aspect of his triumphant and glorious manhood.[1]

The community formed by Balinese men, nature and the gods, the working arrangement of Balinese *subaks, banjars* and *desas*, is a world which seems so complete in itself that there appears to be no need, and indeed no place, for anything else, least of all for the high-pitched voice of politics, for dynastic struggles, state bureaucracies, or rulers.

According to the *babad* chronicles, the lords, princes and kings in fact came from overseas and the splendour of the state was forcedly super-imposed on the Balinese people. According to the most influential among many legends, Majapahit nobles accompanying the Javanese captains on their conquest of Bali built in the fourteenth century the exemplary royal palace in Samprangan. From that *puri* (which was later moved to Gelgel, and in the seventeenth century to Klungkung) the classical Balinese state emerged. The brilliance of royalty radiated from this nucleus throughout the island, creating eventually, by the nine-teenth century, nine glorious princes' or lesser kings' *puris*, dozens of resplendent nobles' houses, all of them considered by their masters to be but dim reflections of the magnificent first Balinese *puri*, or better yet, of the 'original' *kraton*, the imperial palace of Majapahit in the far away Java of the past.

The legend of the foreign origin of Balinese royalty and state was attractive, and Balinese kings and princes and lords cultivated it through the centuries. Even many of the early Western visitors to Bali accepted it at face value. Overhearing the dulcet tones of the *gamelan Semar pengulingan,* or god-of-love orchestra of the royal sleeping quarters, watching royal cremations where, as one eyewitness to such an event in 1847 described it, wives and concubines 'with a mirror in one hand and a comb in the other'[2] were sacrificed on their lords' funeral pyres, it was easy to believe that the nobility originated in another, nobler land, that the blood of royalty, as a *topeng* (drama) libretto proclaims, 'smells fragrant'. In fact, the Balinese state, with its hierarchical structure, is much older than the Majapahit influence, and probably dates from the very early

The baris, ancient ritual dance of virility and, traditionally, royal power, performed in the mountain village of Kintamani.

Balé kulkul – belfry tower of a desa temple at Gelgel. The kulkul, or alarm drum made of a slit, hollowed tree trunk (or of bronze, formerly) has been an attribute of every village, banjar, subak and kingdom. It sounds the alarm at times of calamities and summons people for work and festivals. And it is holy.

centuries of this millennium. It grew out of the natural processes of Balinese development as a civilization, and was an inseparable part of Balinese culture, until it was destroyed in the *puputans* of 1906–8.

Also, the nobles and peasants were not so far removed from each other as legend made it appear. There were inner courts in the Balinese palace which nobody dared to enter except the ruler – and his retinue of clowns, servants, dancers and concubines, an influential group who more often than not came from the village, remained spiritually part of the village, and were outspoken in their peasant wit. The second gate of the palace was kept closed most of the time by a splendid ornate door. But there was rarely a door in the entrance to the outer court, and the walls, moreover, were often intersected, so that people could wander in and out. Certainly, the people were themselves considered to be an embellishment to the palace, and the essence of the state. For every important ceremony, they crowded close to the throne, watching the ruler, chattering, happy and relaxed. The ruler sat on a pedestal, sublime, high above the people, and yet the bustle around him enspirited his power and sustained his position.

Endless walls, high, gilded and richly carved gates, many-tiered pagodas of royal palaces and noble houses – all amidst muddy fields – it was, and still is, a striking sight, and yet not one of disharmony. Each building and each structure fits surprisingly well into the landscape, and every peasant, if allowed, would be able to walk through the inner courts with his eyes bound, without losing his way. Sometimes there was a lily pond, a pleasure garden or a water pavilion in the palace, and nearly always a *balé kerta* where the royal judiciary met, and a special section where corpses of the nobility were kept before cremation. But otherwise, the topological frame of the palace categorically had to be identical with the layout to which every house on the island conformed. Each of the royal courtyards, like every courtyard in Bali, had to be rectangular in shape, with a walled, windowless *gedong* where the principal couple of the family slept, and where money and valuables were often kept. All *balé* houses in the compound, a kitchen, a rice barn, family shrines and a refuse heap, in the palace as in a peasant's house, were ritually and strictly situated along the holy *kaja-kelod* way. Steps or low barriers in the ornate gates between the individual parts of the palace were said to be designed for keeping pigs, imaginary or real, from wandering through the princely courts.

According to legend, a kingdom was once overthrown while its king was absorbed in a cockfight in a village far from the centre of politics where he should have been at the time. Kings, like commoners, loved to keep caged songbirds, they observed the same ceremonies, prayed to the same gods, used the same flowers during worship, even if their offerings were immensely more lavish than those of the peasants – the difference was of quantity, not of kind. We know from ancient *lontars* and from very old people's descriptions that village girls were invited to the palace to be *legong* dancers, and sometimes the most talented and beautiful of them became one of the *raja's* wives, or even the queen. Village and palace music were essentially the same, and after the destruction of the classical Balinese state early in the twentieth century by the Dutch and the *puputans*, it was quite natural for any prince who had survived to join a village orchestra, or to dance the part of a witch or a clown or a hero: the village audience accepted him because he knew their jokes, their ethics, and their tunes.

In *arja*, classical Balinese opera, highborn characters still often speak and sing in *kawi* – the old, half-forgotten, highly ceremonial language of the Majapahit conquerors – but everything they say, whether the *arja* be given

in a *puri* or in a village, is immediately summarized – corrupted, some say – by the servants and clowns and other commoners in the opera. The dialogue is not literally translated into present-day Balinese; rather, the spirit of the play is conveyed, and not rarely it seems that the 'coarse' characters are the main protagonists – that the play is, in fact, theirs. In another genre of Balinese classical drama, the *topeng*, or masked play, the kings, lords and noblemen do not speak at all, and it is up to the people who play the roles of commoners in the play to express all the ideas for their superiors. None of this struck either king or peasant watching the play as strange or unnatural. It was generally accepted, as part of both palace and village culture, that the *raja* needed the people to sustain his image; but the obvious question remains: for what did the people need the *raja*?

Certainly, without the authority of the ruler Balinese agriculture in classical times would not have functioned as smoothly as it did. The water always ran from the mountains to the sea, and passed many *subaks* on its way, self-contained communities – and self-interested, too. There were dry seasons when it would have been the most natural thing in the world for a *subak* in the mountains to consume all the water flowing through its irrigation system, without regard for the *subaks* downstream. Should that happen, the shortage of water, growing worse down towards the sea, would bring drought and famine, epidemics and death. Again, it seemed

77

In the most elevated kaja/east corner of the Klungkung royal puri compound, near the sacred garden, stands a pavilion. There, the high priests held their meetings to decide, in the name of the king, the criminal cases brought before them. The most dreadful oaths were taken by the accused, summoning terrible demons, sending streams of coming generations to thousand-year sufferings in hell. One name by which this court pavilion is known is 'Amrtaghosa', Voice of the Immortals, and a Balinese still can hear the voice when he looks up at the ceiling. The old paintings done in classical 'Kamasan style' did not survive the turbulent times Klungkung passed through. But they have been repeatedly restored, most recently a few years ago by the painters of the Kamasan village, and so the form and spirit of this royal tradition have been kept alive.

natural for a *subak* to avoid the water when the flood came – and to release torrents that could destroy the dikes and fields of the *subaks* lower down the hill. Such problems were more often than not solved in the end by a compromise reached by the adjoining *subaks* concerned. But still calamities occurred, and disputes took place which were unsolvable by the individual irrigation associations. This was the opportunity for a higher authority, a mightier power, to step in and augment the *subak's* means, or correct the *subak's* selfish wisdom.

One of the most important officials of the Balinese king, according to some records, was the *sedahan agung*, a major-domo, rent master, tax collector, keeper of the palace treasury, provider of the *raja's* food, drinks and betel nut. One of the main duties of that steward was the supervision of the fields, particularly the irrigated ones. The *sedahan agung* and his deputies had to keep constant watch over the twists and turns the water took. By appointment of the ruler, it was up to the *sedahans* to find out wherever the interests of a *subak* encroached on the well-being of another (and of course to make sure that the *subaks* were capable of paying their taxes to the king). If a calamity took place or a dispute arose which was beyond a *subak's* capacity to solve (or if the officials were able to convince the peasants that this was the case), it would be the *sedahan* who decided in the ruler's name which river would be diverted, which stream blocked, what proportion of dam water should be apportioned to each of the quarreling *subaks,* and even sometimes which *sawahs* should be sacrificed, and which planted only once over a period of several seasons. The *raja,* through the *sedahan agung,* could in those cases restrain the *subaks* – and stimulate them, too. The Balinese system of irrigation was the invention of the peasants themselves. It was the product of the imagina-tion, initiative, and hard work of individual *subaks,* and then of inter-*subak* agreements. But occasionally a broader sense of perspective and greater means were required. Sometimes an uninvolved person was needed to point out a possibility or to realize it, perhaps the building of a new dam or an enlargement of an irrigation complex. The ruler might reduce the taxes of those peasants who were willing to start the job, or he might even turn the number of peasants required into slaves until the job was done. Any Balinese citizen of a given kingdom might be forced by the ruler to come and help in a task that was beyond the capacity of the few *subaks* immediately concerned.

The classical Balinese state, most scholars agree, was not 'hydraulic despotism', as one scholar described it.[3] The ruler's role in organizing irrigation, and in the peasant economy generally, was largely peripheral, and royal intervention in the *subaks'* or other associations' affairs was rare. But intervention came, as a rule, in moments of deepest crisis for a given community, and it was, therefore, well remembered.

A Balinese ruler was believed to partake of the wisdom of the gods, and because of that, only he could, on a certain day marked in the sacred calendar, order a pilgrimage to be made to the highest lake or spring of the realm. The peasants, if they did not want to invoke the wrath of the gods, the ruler and the future, had to obey the order, to journey upstream, to make an offering and ask for blessing. This was the Opening of Opening Ceremony. Only after the long-awaited signal was given by the king, water-opening rituals in individual valleys and by individual *subaks* might be performed in a strictly ordered time sequence – descending slowly from the mountains to the sea. Not until the king had spoken the word could a new agricultural cycle begin for each *subak*, working in its own complex way.

In agriculture, each Balinese community of classical times tried to be self-contained. This was also true in terms of religion. Yet in this case too the rulers' power, however rarely exercised, was indispensable. There had been a unified state religious cult in classical Bali, symbolized most clearly by the *sadkahyangan*, or 'six sanctuaries', a group of highly respected state (or sometimes provincial) temples.[4] The *sadkahyangan* was oriented according to the sacred *kaja-kelod* axis, containing upperworld temples (usually on the highest mountain of the realm), one or more chthonic

One of the private temples of the surviving Balinese aristocracy in Badung. Family gods in particular have been contacted here, and the old raja still remembers with pride the part he took in the frequent rebuildings of the temple, pointing out the sculptures and reliefs on the walls, gates and shrines he carved himself.

Right: I Gusti Gde Ngurah Pamecutan at the age of eighty-six. Pamecutan was a minor appendage of the Badung princedom in classical times, and its puputan happened only a few hours after the famous puputan of Badung. The raja, who was eleven years old at the time, tells how he was seriously wounded and left on the field. He was covered with bodies, and found when night fell. When he came to, he began to weep, saying 'I want to go home,' but there was no home to go to. Now, with perfect ease and dignity, he lives according to the ethical code of his royal ancestors.

Below: Royal as well as divine sovereignty is acknowledged by white and brightly coloured parasols.

temples (by the sea), and the 'main' temple in the capital or nearby, the *pura penataran agung,* where important state meetings took place, and where the royal court of justice sometimes held its sessions. The spirit of the *sadkahyangan* of the state was the same dynamic triad of gods, devils and men as that of the three main temples of the villages. But the *sadkahyangan* was believed to be more – it was essential to the whole realm. Here royal services were held, and all-state festivals. Here, and only here, those often confusingly diverse village gods of Bali could meet, and here their web of blood relations, their very identity sometimes, could be explained from an all-state perspective. Everyone in a whole province, or even everyone in Bali could, from time to time, make pilgrimages to these holy temples, to pray and have a good time.

Although we cannot say during which century, it must have been before Majapahit and even before the Hindus came that the first Balinese *subak* started on a project so ambitious that it could only be accomplished with the help of a higher authority. And some time in that dim past, the first of the frequent wars among neighbouring *desas* may have come to a stalemate, necessitating an unpleasant compromise and the intervention of a ruler to solve the conflict. Pre-kingdom and supra-village forms – peasant royal prerogatives, *desa* federations, diminutive princedoms, and their piecemeal aggrandizement into kingdoms – are clearly recorded in ancient inscriptions. The Balinese peasants, building their dams, dikes, and *desa* walls, also built the glory of the realm. This should be remembered – otherwise the rich texture of the Balinese royal culture would appear to be simply a baroque superabundance of picturesque paradoxes, sometimes surprisingly fastidious, at other times almost vulgar. The gigantic state ceremonies, the huge royal ritual, can only be understood if we accept the splendour as being the peasants' doing too.

The Balinese classical state has been aptly described as a 'theatre state'.[5] The rulers were patrons of the arts, they favoured actors and musicians, exempted them from taxes, and treasured them as jewels of their realm. Court life was a continuous flow of ritual extravagance. The best artists were engaged and the whole country was invited to watch them, and with them the king. Art filled the courts so absolutely and involved the people flowing through the palace gates so intensely, that the main function of the kingdom appeared to be art. The state moved to music. The public tax went largely for mass rituals. War, in essence and appearance, was a spectacle, sometimes brutish, sometimes stopped as the first man fell dead, but always a performance directed by the king to impress enemies, friends and subjects – all connoisseurs. The death of a nobleman provided the reason for an absolutely astounding celebration, and great cremations cost fortunes, which went up in smoke.

The ruler himself had to be a dazzling work of art. In one reverent eulogy, contained in the northern chronicle, the *Babad Buleleng,* the king is compared to a *gamelan* orchestra. Another king, according to a *topeng* play proved himself the ruler by majestic dancing. Dance was power, and it was inevitable part of every prince's education to learn several dances in a supremely professional manner, as well as the art of carving, playing *gamelan* music, and reciting or singing classical verses:

> . . . the kings and princes were the impresarios, the priests the directors, the peasantry the supporting cast, stage crew, and audience. The stupendous cremations, teeth-filings, temple dedications, the pilgrimages and blood sacrifices, mobilizing hundreds, even thousands of people and great quantities of wealth, were not means to political ends, they were the ends themselves, they were what the state was for.[6]

The king was the leading actor, and notions of the ruler's supremacy appealed to the Balinese people as only aesthetical images could. The state was the standard of elegance. The Balinese ruler was revered as a god. He appeared seated on the *padmasana,* or lotus seat, and offerings were brought to him in the same way that they are proffered to the gods to this day by *pendet* dancers. Divine epithets were included among his royal titles, and participation of a commoner in a state ceremony was described by the same term as was service at a religious festival. Rulers were held aloof from the *mertyapada,* or world of human beings, and were worshipped in every village throughout the realm. The Balinese peasants were firmly convinced that, like gods and devils, the kings should be intensively invoked, worshipped, and thus controlled, by ritual means.

A Balinese village still impresses some Westerners as being 'chivalric' or 'troubadorial'.[7] In former times, a peasant was perfectly willing to crouch, or prostrate himself, before a ruler. The peasants were eager subjects, and made an enthusiastic audience. But they only did what an expert audience might be expected to do: they could not dismiss a ruler as they could dismiss a *klian* of their *subak* or *banjar* if he made a mistake, yet still they were alert. They enjoyed the play, admired the principal actor – and watched carefully to be sure that the crucial line between limelight and daylight was never trespassed. Actors off the stage are often pitiful. The Balinese idolized their rulers as actors, and in the same way that they still worship their demons and gods – in order to enhance their splendour, encourage their self-absorption, and keep them

These nineteenth-century doors from royal compounds in North Bali, richly carved, painted and gilded (below and overleaf above), were a major attraction of the raja's or prince's private quarters. The doors, almost like temple gates, were considered not merely functional, but as a magically charged threshold between safety and a demonic 'outside'. The carving was often closely related to temple reliefs and sculptures.

Below: Wisnu on his mount, Garuda. A pillar-base, once mounted in the centre of the ridge-pole, high up under the roof of a pavilion. The god, seated on his mount, looked down upon his people, so it would not have been appropriate to place him at the base of the pillar, next to the ground.

at a measured distance from the everyday world.

Bali is a marvel of the miniature. Consider the particular beauty of the ricefields, so complex in design, yet accomplished within a framework so diminutive, on a scale so remarkably intimate. This is partly because the rugged landscape defies any attempt at uniformity; it may be an aspect of the famous Balinese artistic skill. But surely the uniqueness of each individual *sawah* is also a manifestation of the way the Balinese eluded any attempt by the king to impose conformity on his subjects.

Not even two villages with identical constitutions existed in Bali. It seemed almost deliberate, as if to confuse the ruler and foil any of his efforts at unified rule. On the other hand, in each *desa* constitution (*awig-awig*) an almost obligatory proud paragraph appeared which said that, 'these rules were set down by the village council, and also observed by the king' (*Awig-awig wikrama desa adat Aan*).[8]

The amazing variety and exhaustive detail of village constitutions in Bali was due, among other things, to the peasants' obsession with not leaving any of the community's problems unsolved, that is, not placing it in a realm where the ruler could and should intervene. Countless conditions were attached to the propriety of a ruler's being able to enter the fray and act as judiciary. Only if a suspect or apprehended criminal

Windows of the inner compounds of puris were also viewed as magical dividing lines. A wooden window panel, depicting a vase surrounded by cloud scrolls and moon and sun. A Balinese version of a Chinese composition; the flower is a Chinese rose. Set in the wall and viewed from inside the room in shadow-puppet performance style, light is carved into a negative image. Central or south Bali, nineteenth century.

Hanuman fighting a demon, a scene from the 'Ramayana'. Wooden window panel, central or south Bali, nineteenth century.

Above and right: Possibly Supraba, a lovely nymph who, from time to time, is sent to earth to test ascetics by trying to tempt them. Her body is entwined in lush vegetation, suggesting seductiveness and fertility.

85

'does not stop, if he does not pay any attention to the congregation,' if he refuses to swear and thus prove his innocence or regret, 'if he does not follow all the time the rules which bring about the well-being of the village, if he ignores them with the result that the old customs are ruined, and if he persists in this disobeying' – only then 'he may be tied and delivered to the king' (*Awig-awig wikrama desa Aan*). Each 'if' deleted would be a broken wall, a blow to the village's dignity. There was no word of the highest or ultimate justice being ordained by the ruling of the king. The lord got what was 'beyond', what the community had thrown away.

In Bali, one's village is the world. Beyond the village is another world – even if it is part of the same province. The rhythm of the *kulkul* drums illustrates this. Even today, the *kulkul* drums of every *desa* send out intricate messages which cannot be understood by anyone from another village – messages concerning such day-to-day activities as agriculture, ceremonial events, and anything else of concern to the village at large. Only a very few drum rhythms are universal in Bali (one being 'Fire!'). There was nothing much like an all-state village civil code in classical Bali, no grandly conceived and recognized system of social security for a Balinese peasant outside his village walls. But neither was there much unrestrained exercise of royal power. Rather loose ties existed between the state and local communities and associations, and a measured distance was guarded carefully by all sides. The ruler could order his subjects to help him with the projects that were beyond the village walls – to fight a dynastic war, to build a royal palace, to pay taxes, out of which all-state ceremonies could be paid for – but he did not 'own' a community. It was rather usual for a king to delegate or give a majority of his kingdom to lesser lords or officials, and there was rarely a lord who could claim more than a minority of a village's citizens as his subjects. Neighbours, or even brothers, might be, and often were, subjects of different lords, and in the frontier areas even of different kings. A commoner might owe military or ritual duty to one lord, pay tax to another, and work as a sharecropper for a third. Instead of communities, it was only some of the individuals, some of the individual households, or rather some of the household's services, which were subject to the kings' and lords' wishes.[9] And if a lord wanted to influence a village community as a whole, to interfere in a community constitution, to use it or change it, he could do so, and often did – but only as the community's, *desa's* or *subak's* ordinary citizen, enjoying an ordinary citizen's rights and being bound by the ordinary citizen's duties.

Each community in Bali seemed to live safely only by keeping the social strain at a high pitch, by constantly disturbing the stability of neighbours and of superiors. The village world of Bali was excessively dynamic and unpredictable; the state structure built upon it was even more shaky and insecure.

> Details aside, the final (that is, nineteenth century) result was an acrobat's pyramid of 'kingdoms' of varying degrees of substantial autonomy and effective power, the main lords of Bali holding the paramount lord upon their shoulders and standing in turn upon the shoulders of the lords whose status was derivative from their own as theirs was from him, and so on down the line.[10]

Not one of the acrobats could be sure of his position, all balanced on the trembling shoulders of those below; and the lowest stood on the volatile earth. Each member of the pyramid was straining against his neighbour, and perhaps the strain was the only thing they had in common besides a vague feeling that a pyramid as marvellous as that should last.

The lesser lords and lords' officials standing immediately 'on peasant shoulders' resonated the tremor of the village world, and conveyed it up to the higher levels of the pyramid, magnifying it by injecting their own petty or noble interests and ambitions into it. In an effort to calm the village, the lords very often invited selected commoners into their courts, and their daughters into their harems. As it was not exceptional for a king to choose a wife of common origin, neither was it unusual for a commoner, an upstart, to inspire his king, or even to establish a new kingdom and a new dynasty.[11]

Peasants at the base of the pyramid danced their own dance, radiating unquiet throughout the structure. Still, their restlessness, dynamism, ambitions, were anchored to the ground, metaphorically, and in reality too, to the ricefields, to village parochialism, to the eternal and predestined cycle of communal life. The lords' movements had very little anchorage. They were only loosely connected with the village, with the *sawahs*. They were less constrained in their outlook and movement, and their sway on the peasant shoulders (so to speak) had a wider range; it seemed almost boundless, and was much more dangerous.

If there were very few norms of inter-*desa* or inter-*subak* relations at village level, there were even fewer concerning generally acceptable etiquette between individual lords, rulers and their realms. Each *raja* or lord was obsessed by his own preconceived pattern of *politesse*, strictly demanding others to pay their respects in a minutely detailed form. Politics of vanity. But the protocol differed for each kingdom, each province, and often was proclaimed by the ruler just for a day, chosen at random, by reading omens in cockfights or in changes in the weather. There was a vast multitude of acts by which one lord could mortally offend another, while, at the same time, no one could say in advance exactly which act would be potentially explosive. The closer two rulers came, the greater the danger that they would clash. The more elaborate the treaty signed by two rulers, the greater the likelihood of it including an offence, of something being overlooked, of it even being the cause of war. Peril was always imminent, and the lords of classical Bali – most of them blood relatives – loved to find excuses for meeting with one

In masked performances, aristocratic figures, wearing complete masks with rigid lower jaws, can scarcely talk at all. Their intentions are expressed by their servants, who wear half masks or masks with movable jaws.

Above: A royal mask of the 'strong and coarse', type (as opposed to the 'refined and sweet' type). Royal masks often were carved by kings themselves, and are today carved by their descendants.

Left: Demonic mask used in the wayang wong (masked 'human-puppet' drama).

Above left: Half mask of a pock-marked servant woman.

another. Writing elaborate and complicated treaties was one of their greatest pleasures: 'The treaties maintained, in such a way, a sense that the perfect system of integration always lay just barely out of reach, prevented from realization only by the duplicity of this lord or the obstinacy of that one.'[12] Balinese history from the sixteenth to the nineteenth century went through a succession of noble meetings, intricate treaties and irate conflicts. Countless bloody wars were waged between rulers and lords and lords' vassals for reasons that would appear petty and trivial to a stranger. Real acts of aggression of course, might be a reason for war, but wars were also waged over an escaped thief, a crooked smile, the wrong order of epithets in an otherwise most devotional letter, an offensive number of roofs on a cremation tower in an otherwise perfect and pleasing funeral ceremony. These were not, in most cases, mere formal pretexts for senseless wars. The wars were ceremonial solutions of real tensions and real problems. Whatever the ostensible cause, and whoever won, the wars appeared to be effective, useful and surprisingly satisfactory to all the warring sides. They were stylized, like a theatre performance,[13] or a hazardous dance of the pyramid of dancing bodies – neighbour testing neighbour in the pyramid, feeling his presence, making sure that he was still there by moving and forcing him to move.

This, then, was the classical Balinese state. Dozens, and from time to time over a hundred lesser and greater lords challenged their superiors and their king. There always had been several kings in Bali, proudly independent and in almost a permanent state of mutual war. And above them was the king of Bali, the paramount lord, the most splendid jewel of the Balinese state, and the precarious pyramid's 'most tremulous peak'.[14]

Performers dancing on each other's shoulders, or building a pyramid of dancing bodies, is a well-known feature of Balinese theatrical art, of the ancient *sanghyang dedari*, for instance, or the modern *janger*. The Balinese do not appear to distinguish much between the physical, social and ethical. To be elevated, whether in dance, in spirit or in politics, means to be exposed, exposed to the threat of imbalance and of a fall. Dancers and

Top: Barong Bangkung, boar's head mask.

Above: Barong Gajah, elephant's head mask.

Right: Type of spinning-wheel which would formerly have been used at a royal wedding, for a bride had to prove that she could cook, weave and spin. Gianyar, twentieth century.

rulers of classical Bali performed and balanced, and the people watched them in awe. Everybody watching appeared to be magnetized, drawn closer to the stage. The awe enriched and actually elevated. The idea of the Balinese state lasted because it made every Balinese excitingly aware of this equilibrium, which the people created together, and of the threats which they averted together, aware of their common fragility and of the laws of insecurity that bound them together. Watching the performance was meant to be the same as participating in it; people were to be made to feel the elevation, the unbalance, the tension, the omnipresent peril of the disruption of the state and the fall of the pyramid.

So what a good ruler was supposed to do was, in fact, to act dramatically, or even more than that, theatrically. A Balinese king was expected to perform in the same way as the *baris* actor described at the beginning of this chapter. His political action was to be a 'test of the power of his wide-opened eyes', an 'admiration of his hands', a 'display of another aspect of his triumphant and glorious manhood'. This was one of the most impressive paradoxes of the classical Balinese culture: only through being an exhibitionist could the ruler be considered truly social.

THE TIME OF
TRANCE

*He rings the bell louder and quicker and stops suddenly . . . gives signs of the
oncoming trance; he gasps, his eyes roll back and his movements take on a tense,
unearthly air . . . he trembles all over and, rolling his eyes in ecstasy, he pronounces the prayers 'for the world' in a deep, strangely changed voice.*[1]

A Balinese baby, from its first moment of awareness, is subjected to a
tender and enervating care. 'Everyone joins in the mild, titillating
teasing of little babies, flipping their fingers, their toes, their genitals,
threatening them playfully, disregarding the sanctity of their heads . . .'[2]
Corpses are 'teased' too – *badés*, towers in which the body is carried to the
cremation ground and which one might expect to be a final resting place
before extinction, are shaken wildly on the way, whirled and twisted and
fought for in passionate play by the excited mourners.

Balinese life is rarely serene. Elopement is still one of the most usual
forms of marriage. Lovers are compared to fighting cocks and the cockfight, at least until very recently, was the most popular pastime in Bali. The
political and social system of classical Bali, as we have seen, kept its
balance through an incessant competition of all the system's component
parts. In their religious practices, the Balinese propitiate demons as well
as gods, and frequently provoke all of them into battle. The essence of
Balinese classical beauty is a drumming alarm, a drama, *ramé*, a joyful
scramble, much the same perhaps, today, as it has been for a thousand
years. A mood of disturbance and ever-surprising syncopes of disquieting rhythm fill the *wayang* theatre, the *gamelan* music, and the
legong dance, which is the embodiment of flashing, highly strung Balinese
grace.

On the other hand, there could hardly be more complex and authoritative laws than the Balinese rules of ethics and politics; Balinese music is
bound by elaborate categorical metric designs, and the dance figures are
minutely prescribed in the old *lontars*, as are the movements of society
itself. The striking beauty of Balinese life and art is disturbing because it is
dynamic and sensitive, but at the same time, tightly restricted. All the
Balinese expressiveness is still understatement, and restless tension lends
grace to the trembling form.

Occasionally, it seems that one explicit word or line or deed is enough
to start an explosion. An elopement, and the theatrical anger of the bride's
kin that is expected to follow, may suddenly erupt into the killing of the

*Rangda, the terrible witch, with the anteng, the white cloth which is her fearful
weapon, in her right hand. The split gate looms behind her in the darkness.*

91

Top: Sunset in Bali is an immense relief after the hot day. But the dramatic shadows of palm trees suggest that demons and witches emerge with darkness.

Above: The monsters should be appeased. The pemangku prays for the night to be blessed.

Opposite: Night falls.

potential groom. A cockfight may be the cause of a communal conflict, a kingdom may be shattered in a *puputan*. The whole island sometimes explodes in a frenzy of hate, or just the white of a dancer's eyes grows wider, a woman falls backward from the brazier and gives a strange unearthly scream, the *gamelan* plays the mad *gegilakan* or the monotonous *batel*, and flowers fall from the dancer's hair. This is the time of trance, and now it seems that the threshold has been crossed.

The best-known occasion when trance dominates the scene is the performance of Rangda, whether in the *Calonarang* play, or in her fight with the Barong. At this ceremony, trance is almost inevitable. Rangda often falls into trance as soon as she does the first steps of her dance, and the two men who impersonate the Barong soon become entranced as well. The Barong's followers generally enter in an elaborate dance formation; they play in groups, or pairs, or sometimes each by himself. But sooner or later, they too go into trance, almost as a rule. They try to stab Rangda, and then, thrown back on themselves by her power, they stab their own bodies. Often at this stage of *ngurek* the *gamelan* players and the audience fall into trance as well.

A very different trance dance is *sanghyang dedari*, in which pre-adolescent girls receive the spirits of *sanghyangs*, or deities, in this case, heavenly nymphs. They are chosen for their proneness to trance by a *pemangku*, and they are trained by going nightly to a temple where, strongly influenced by the chanting of a chorus and by fumes of incense, they become more and more susceptible to receiving the spirits of the nymphs. The little girls are trained in no other way, and have never formally danced. When they are able to go into trance, the real performance is given. At that time, they wear elaborate headdresses and a beautiful apron is sometimes given to them, along with a little fan. They dance – marvellously indeed, a sort of relaxed variation on the complicated *legong* themes which they have never studied, and which normally take months of hard work to memorize. The little *sanghyangs* perform on the shoulders of adult men, dreamily arching their slim bodies back and forth, from side to side, at dangerous angles; sometimes they dance on the ground, solo and in pair, with their eyes closed, but still in a tense contrapuntal relation with the partner.

Kecak is a male performance. The men, naked except for a loincloth and a flower behind the ear, squat in a mass of closely packed bodies in a circle around a solo dancer – the trancer. They all chant and sway to the rhythm of the chant, like an undersea flower, the flower suddenly exploding as they shoot up their hands, fingers outstretched to their limits, the chant bursting in toad-like shouts that gave the *kecak* its name. The man in the middle dances as if aloof from the mass, he towers above them, sometimes provokes them, sometimes fights with them, until, with an infinitely slow and dramatic motion he merges into the now generally entranced crowd. In some parts of Bali, under Hindu influence, the *kecak* was incorporated into a scene from the *Ramayana*, in which the *kecak* chorus became an army of monkeys preparing for battle. But this Hinduized version appears never to have been more than a superficial layer imposed on a pre-Hindu male chorus, unchanged through the millennium.

Balinese animal trances may be even more ancient that the *kecak*. An outsider is rarely allowed to see them, and they are generally performed in the more remote parts of the island. In contrast to the *ngurek, kecak* and *sanghyang dedari*, animal trances have almost nothing in common with dance. They are rather crude happenings, and sometimes frighteningly

violent. There are various types of animal trances, depending upon which spirit enters a man – it may be a toad, or a pig, a monkey, snake or tiger. Indeed, men are sometimes entered even by the spirit of a potato, a rice-pounding mortar, or a potlid.[3]

A distinctly Balinese notion that every part of the body has the potential for a separate existence is given substance in another very strange form of trance. Only a hand or arm of a man is possessed, while the man himself watches it, throughout the twenty or thirty minutes the trance lasts, with horror in his eyes.

It has been said that a 'hobby-horse dream' of childhood[4] is performed in the *sanghyang jaran,* or 'spirit of the horse' trance, when a man rides a stick with a palm-leaf tail and a horse's head carved in wood, until he goes into a sometimes violent trance.

A tendency towards trance seems to be contained in the most various manifestations of Balinese behaviour, particularly in acts oriented outwards, towards the community. 'There is a sense in which it would be true to say that all dancing in Bali is related to trance consciousness.'[5] The performers often dance themselves into trance, while the musicians too may play themselves into a state of trance. The Balinese *topeng* actor seems to be able to enter into the character which his mask represents only while in trance, and the Balinese audience, at great ceremonies and temple

festivals, appears frequently to be, if not entranced, then just on the brink of trance.

It would seem that the inclination towards trance is a permanent undercurrent of the Balinese consciousness, and a functional component of the Balinese character. Yet when it comes to dominate, strangely enough, the undercurrent, the component, seems to flood the consciousness, to blow the structure all to bits, to turn the behaviour patterns of the Balinese into their reverse.

These timid and mild people, so often with 'I do not dare' on their lips, now, in time of trance, suddenly reveal an extravagance of bravery. Docile young girls of six, when entranced and dancing as *sanghyang dedari*, become capricious if not cruel with the men who care for them. Distinguished among world cultures by their body consciousness, so sensitive to every touch, in trance, for instance during *ngurek,* the Balinese appear all at once to be tough, mindless of pain. They stab themselves, or they may force burning coals into their mouths, and lick the fire.

'The clouds have red edges, a rain of blood falls', entranced men chant in the *kecak* chorus. They are Fiend Dancers at Trance now, the terrible Durga's servants, listed in *Purwa Bhumi*. Usually so modest in their eating habits, while in trance they eat living chickens with macabre relish. So apprehensive in their normal state of mind, of such balanced poise, now

Above: Masks are brought to the temple, and the pemangku revitalizes them.

Below: Next dancers – heavenly nymphs – may enter, or other kinds of dance and drama may be performed to entertain the audience.

Opposite: Finally, Barong appears, and the main performance begins.

Opposite and right: Dance of a royal pair in a scene from a Hindu epic.

Below: A pair of straight-bladed krises. The gold embellishment on the left handle is the holy singa, symbol of strength. It is from a Brahmana-Boddha family of Karangasam, east Bali.

they cry for every imaginable perversion of the equilibrium. They enjoy *paling,* being dizzied, disoriented. Indeed, *paling* is one of the many terms for trance: people in trance are exultantly disoriented; lost in space, they wildly bend their bodies in what in a normal state would be considered a blasphemous effort to put the head lower than the abdomen. Or they sway limply to and fro in an equally indecent way, like boats in a storm, like boats on the brink of sinking.

Taboos are broken by a Balinese in trance, and it seems the most sacred taboos are broken with the greatest zeal. During *ngurek,* when trancers are not trying to stab Rangda or themselves, they point their daggers at the shrines, or try to climb up and put their dirty feet on the holy temple roofs. The most authoritative *kaja-kelod* axis of Balinese piety means nothing now. Caste has no meaning in trance, and this is perhaps the only occasion when a member of the *triwangsa* may speak in deferential, self-deprecating language to a commoner. Age is not revered, and an old woman may become a girl, immensely relishing her girlishness.

Sex barriers are assailed during the time of trance. A man can be seen decked with women's bracelets and weeping in a feminine voice, or a woman may sit cross-legged like a man and speak in a hoarse voice. In the normal state of mind, sexual intercourse on a temple ground is something too horrible for the Balinese even to imagine, and if such a thing should be discovered, some village constitutions still order that the guilty man 'is to be castrated, the girl to be taken to the graveyard and here a hot poker inserted into her vagina . . . the *pura* [temple] must be torn down and thrown into the sea.' (*Awig-awig wikrama desa adat Aan*). This is for everyday life. But during the time of trance, and on the very temple ground, the two sexes get themselves into a close physical contact, much closer than would usually be thought decent.[6] Sexuality may become blatant and rampant. Women arch their bodies, bellies lifted, legs spread wide, some go into a spasmodic rhythm of convulsion, their screaming and moaning 'akin to a sexual excitement which can render no appeasement.'[7]

Even animalism and sodomy, considered the worst crimes in Bali, are flirted with. Sometimes animal trances are a kind of light play of nostalgia for the purely natural life that has passed away even for the Balinese. 'When I'm a *sanghyang* snake suddenly my thoughts are delicious. Thus my feelings (*baju*) being delicious, suddenly I see something like forests, woods, with many, many trees. When my body is like that, as a snake, my feeling (*rasa*) is of going through the woods and I am pleased.'[8] 'Monkeymen' climb high to the tree-tops during their trances, exhibiting extraordinary feats of monkey acrobatics, jumping down on all fours before being caught, restrained, and brought back to normal. 'Dog-men' bark, 'snakemen' snake, 'toad-men' croak. But often, animal trances are much cruder, as when a pig-man wallows with relish in the mud, drinks from a stone trough, builds a nest out of dry leaves in the corner reserved for pigs, and, if in the mood, tries to mount a 'sow' (woman) or a sow within his reach.

There is a tendency to all that even during many of the non-trance performances. On stage, much is allowed that would not be possible in everyday life – the theatrical caricature of status, clowns aping their masters to the mirth of the audience, a theatrical caricature of balance, theatrical passions, love, anger and violence – 'exaggeration of those emotions which, outside the stage, no adult Balinese display'.[9] During the trance, this is all only a few degrees stronger, a short step more explicit.

Trance excitement and trance hysterics are due to a communal psychosis and a passion for the play, but also, perhaps, to the omnipresent and generally felt threat. There are stories of trances breaking the bonds (and an outside observer may frequently be supplied with them on the evening before a trance is due to happen, possibly as a sort of warming-up exercise); stories not of ancient times, and not pleasant to remember, of a whole village or even a larger community entranced and running amok, of Rangda disappearing into the darkness forever; a story of a 'pig-man' escaping from the court where he was playing, roaming the streets, ravaging the gardens, eating the plants, 'which was not good for the village', eating large quantities of filth he found in the roadways, 'which was not good for him'.[10] 'Those become *sanghyang* who are bold,' the Balinese say.

To feel the threshold, it would seem, is the most important experience of everybody present at a trance event, and maybe even the main reason why the trance happens.[11] One senses that even at the most abandoned trance, something must be left unsaid, or undone. In the middle of a step or in the middle of a word, madness should be avoided, the spear of horror broken. There is a Balinese belief that fear can be reduced by taking off one's sarong and shaking it out. The trance appears to follow a similar pattern.

It was a very strange experience to see her [a *sanghyang dedari* trancer] dance without contact of her eyes with the world around her. She danced in a dream from which one felt infinitely remote, and when the music stopped one almost longed for her release; that she might sink down and pass completely into a trance world of isolation. But this never happened.[12]

A man, woman, or child in trance, like a good actor, should never

Above: A temple dance preceding the appearance of the Barong.

Below: A pair of krises with silver and gold handles in the shape of Raksasas, here guarding against demons. The flame-like blades are ancient, the handles of a later date. They belonged to a Satria family of Singaraja.

step out of the limelight. The trance should never be the act of a loner in Bali. On the contrary, a large crowd should always be present, enjoying the trance and watching closely. Whenever a trancer, under the strain he has invoked, appears to be about to 'go mad' (for which the Balinese language has terms quite different from those for trance) – the whole community, with priests and officials leading the way, rushes forward; some apply holy water, sometimes a brazier, others suck at the blood or put a hibiscus on the wound if the *kris* has pierced the skin during *ngurek*. Tenderly if possible, brutally if necessary, the trancer is brought back to normalcy. And more than once in the past a trancer who broke all bounds was killed by his kin, mercilessly, as though he were a beast.

Trances are not expected to take place except on ceremonial occasions, and essentially, the trance is a communal play. According to some village constitutions, to fake a trance is a crime against the community. There is even something of a puppet quality in the way the Balinese act in trance. They are actually 'put' into trance by the chanting and dancing of the whole community as much as by the incense, and they are directed by the community throughout the play. There is nothing unusual in an old lady excusing herself seconds before plunging into a deep trance, saying, 'I am going to work'. Trancers – violent, frenzied, infantile – 'work' in the service of their community, and are duly respected for it.

To enter trance in Bali is *nadi*, which also means 'to create', 'to become', 'to exist'. In some villages, when people fall into a trance, the community exclaims, '*kerauhan*' – they are entered – and the people often sit down at that moment so as to be lower than those entranced, who are now closer to the divine than everybody else. Even the proud priests sit down. *Sanghyang dedari* dancers are addressed '*ratu*', your highness, in some villages. And in some, trancers are *pelinggihan*, the thrones of the gods, or the pillars of the gods, all of them, even the animal trancers, considered to be an honour to the community by their very presence there.

If a community, or a kingdom in former times, was in trouble, it was often a trancer, or the god in him, who was called to solve the problem. Sometimes he would dictate an ordinary solution or he might lay down a whole new set of rules or ceremonies; sometimes he would even announce a new set of gods to worship, and a new myth.[13] *Sanghyang dedari* was, it appears, originally performed only when a pestilence or other dreadful calamity threatened the village. The trance was believed to be the remedy. There was a remarkable, shocking, and, the Balinese would say, effective revival of trances throughout the island eighty years ago, at the culmination of the Dutch conquest, forty years ago, when the war and revolution reached the island in full force, twenty years ago when there was a plague of rats, the holy Gunung Agung erupted, and the Indonesian state rocked in the deepest crisis of its independent existence. By means of trance, the Balinese, throughout their history, tried to defend their integrity, mental as well as social. And there are many reasons to believe that those light-minded and pragmatic people are still ready to stage scenes of mass hysteria whenever their village or their island is under strain, now or in the future.

One might think that too great a risk is involved when a trancer – almost a baby sometimes, a person seemingly unbalanced, often – dictates a course of action, and whatever he says is obeyed by his community as though it were a command from on high. But actually, the danger is never too grave, precisely because trance is a communal play. The trancer is in the centre of the communal stage. Balinese rules being so strict, it often seems that only the trancer – similar now to the Balinese ruler on top of the precarious pyramids of state – may defy the code. Like the ruler, the trancer is exposed for everybody to see: he is daring, he is close to the threshold, close to the fall, less anchored and, like the ruler, freer and therefore better empowered to pronounce new, even revolutionary words. In Bali, 'trance makes change possible'.[14]

Rehearsals always attracted more attention among the Balinese than final performances, which are redolent of perfection, and therefore impasse. Balinese civilization, like the Balinese *gamelan*, even at the classical heights of the fifteenth to the nineteenth century, sounded faintly out of tune. The Balinese needed the discord to move into a change that brought the music towards an ideal, absolutely harmonious but never to be fully attained.

Bali has grown to old age, but nothing has ever been more transient than Balinese art. The masterpieces made of palm leaves, to choose only one example, how eagerly would they be accepted by any Western museum or art gallery, and how carefully would they be handled – if only the jewels were not dried up and spoiled a day or two after being so painstakingly created. Beauty has never been measured in Bali by the length of time it lasted, but rather by its proximity to the ideal, by the intensity of the creative moment.

Perhaps the split gate, built of soft stone on that trembling earth, was always Bali's best – the halting prayer, the broken finger pointing to heaven, the shattered rock, heavy on the ground, yet still a flame in its shape and meaning. Watching a trance, forgetting for that moment all the changes which have taken place in this century, the essence of Bali

Above: On the high tide of trance, and beyond the brink. The entranced old women (above) are appreciated and closely watched by the community.

still seems to be the flame itself, and the smoke of incense rising from the fire, fading into air, and thus, only thus, acquiring the right quality to become the steep and hazardous staircase to the gods.

Trance in Bali is not madness, it is not drunkenness, and no sense of hangover follows it. 'After the trance is over, the women's hair is twined again on their heads – as is done during childbirth to calm them.'[15] Each trancer, after being brought back to himself, pays reverence to a shrine, begs the gods for permission to leave, to take a bath, or settles down right away to discuss his share in the offerings or some other business as though he were unrelated to the violence, darkness and fury he has just left. He, like the rest of the community, is calm and relaxed, as if no trance had taken place. Or perhaps it would be more accurate to say that his serenity is a result of the fact that the trance did happen, proceeded as it should, and, in a proper fashion, is over.

Nobody should be hurt during trance, no real sex act committed, no shrine desecrated. The trance should be very much like a play – enacted, but as intensely and solemnly as if the success of each performance were a matter of life and death. And actually, by the Balinese way of seeing things, it is. Through the trance, the Balinese are challenging the limits of their individual and social existence. They play with fire, and find courage and self-confidence in the adventure. They try to prevent a danger by making it alarming before it is too late. They try to avoid a catastrophe by performing it, by letting everybody feel it, and live through it, on the stage, and while there is still time.

The man possessed by Rangda, (left), who has overstepped the limit, is countered by the non-tranced villagers, not with krises or in the ceremonial way Rangda is usually dealt with, but without any respect, quickly, as an abnormal or sick person would be dealt with.

Above: The king's minister in the drama of 'Calonarang' challenges Rangda. He is still in his human form but soon, in anger, will change into the Barong. Right: The scene that immediately follows: the ribald clowns are talking about how nice it is to be safe, now and forever; the witch, Rangda, is actually already behind them, preparing to strike them down.

Above: Detail of the blade of the left kris on page 99. The gold embellishment shows Saraswati, goddess of learning, on her mount.

THE IMAGES

Balinese art can be compared to amber, which, through its inclusion of foreign bodies, achieves an unrepeatable beauty. The classic Balinese art of the last few centuries is the result of a process of assimilation of indigenous art forms with forms introduced from outside. During the course of a thousand years, these foreign elements were adapted to suit native requirements, thus giving rise to an autonomous art. It is the maturity of these combined elements and the magnificent richness of their expression which give rise to a recognizably Balinese art. In this chapter, a few examples illustrating different artistic tendencies will be discussed.

The earliest evidence of native Balinese craftsmanship includes neolithic stone implements, megalithic menhirs (ancient monumental standing stones) and several small step-pyramids resembling in shape and design some of the pyramids of Java and the Polynesian archipelago. Balinese bronze age culture is documented by many beautiful objects, such as ceremonial axes, shovels, weapons, necklaces, buckles and other ornamental articles.

The most conspicuous in the array of bronze artefacts are giant kettle-drums of the so-called Dongson type (the name derives from the original place of discovery in present-day Vietnam). Similar instruments were found in different parts of China and in other countries of Southeast Asia. Several kettle-drums of this type have also been discovered in Indonesia. They are interesting both as evidence of cultural history and as examples of a highly distinctive style and craftsmanship. Considering their remarkable size and surface ornamentation, they can be regarded as major achievements of earliest metallurgy, not only in Bali, but in the world.

Bali possesses the biggest object of this kind yet discovered – the 'Moon of Bali' or the 'Moon of Pejeng'. This is a drum or, more precisely, a kettle-shaped gong of giant proportions. The cylindrical body measures 186.5 centimetres in length and the resonating disc has a diameter of 160 centimetres. This gong is preserved in the ancient Pura Panataran Sasih temple at Pejeng, the former residential city where it was discovered.

Whether this object was imported to Bali or manufactured by native craftsmen remains a matter of conjecture. The gong could have been cast by the *cire-perdue* technique or a multiple stone mould might have been employed. Fragments of a stone mould were actually found near the original place of discovery, but although they are of the same type, and similarly ornamented, these fragments could not have been used to mould the Moon of Pejeng, because they are too small. Nevertheless, they are evidence that other, similar gongs were cast in Bali.

Archaeologists trace the origin of the 'Moon of Pejeng' back to the first or even third century BC. The original purpose of the gong, like the symbolic meaning of its ornamentation, is steeped in mystery. The cylindrical body of this remarkable instrument is adorned with simple geometrical band-ornamentation consisting of straight lines and triangles (this motif, known as *tumpal*, is still frequent in Indonesian art). A pair of mask-like faces fills the space between the handles. The resonating disc is decorated with characteristic curving patterns which, like the centrally placed eight-pointed star, also occur in some of the smaller instruments of the Dongson type.

It seems very likely that this no doubt sacral instrument served ritual purposes and it was probably used in ceremonies in which water (life-sustenance) and astral aspects played their part. Whatever the original significance of the symbolism may be, the anthropomorphic masks are among the earliest of their kind in Indonesia.[1] One leading scholar described the 'Moon of Pejeng' as 'one of the most magnificent creations of mankind'.[2]

It is paradoxical and yet symptomatic that a small territory like Bali could produce works of art so numerous, large, yet at the same time exquisitely *bijou*-like, compared to similar works produced by much larger cultural areas either in Asia or other continents.

As rice grows and matures it changes colour and the Balinese have names for every stage. The last and most important is the stage when the rice is golden brown, and it is called 'pregnant'. Above: Over this archaic amphitheatre the sun performs an ancient rite: promising the young, green rice the colour of gold. Right: rice terraces next to the royal candi of Tampaksiring above the holy river Pakerisan. Left: Shadow puppet of the serpent Antaboga, made c. 1800 at Klungkung.

There is a view which finds ardent supporters among today's practitioners of applied arts and architecture, that a work of art should combine functional simplicity with aesthetic value. This ideal is fully realized in the earliest and most impressive works of art native to Bali – the ricefield terraces of the *sawah*-culture.

In these terraces a symbiosis was achieved of man and nature – one which did not result in the devastation of the countryside, but, on the contrary, gave rise to an almost ideal synthesis of those two aspects distinctive of much genuine art – function and beauty.

Although scholars are divided as to the chronology of events that led up to the creation of this monumental sculpture which girds the entire island, it is certain that the *sawah* terraces represent one of the earliest expressions of Balinese creativity and that their functionalism and aesthetic appeal have passed the test of centuries.

Confronted with this giant sculpture that lives on in space and time as the work of countless human generations, a contemporary observer is bound to reflect on the true value of human labour. It is interesting to compare this marvellous work of art with a rather different 'monumental work' expressive of the 'creative aspirations' of our age – rocks wrapped in foil.[3]

Perhaps all one can do is address a humble plea to Surya, the sun god whose life-giving powers are invoked by every Balinese, to hold his protective hand in the days to come over a creation which, so full of life and beauty, yet affords sustenance to millions. If we appeal to his generosity and benevolence, he might perhaps close his eyes to the human folly of our days.

Many a flourishing civilization of the past was eclipsed just because it violated man's balanced relationship with nature. Elsewhere the sad remnants of architecture, of sculpture and sometimes even literature are eloquent testimony to the inexorable logic of cultural decline.

In Bali, men fashioned a masterpiece out of such unlikely substances as fertile mud and flowing water, so difficult to control and to maintain. Taken together, the ricefield terraces constitute an exquisite work of art which permanently mirrors the essential harmony between the human mind and nature, a harmony forever created and recreated in a process of never-ending transformation.

A brief description of the physical contour-map of Bali covering a territory of approximately 5,500 square kilometres would probably run as follows: Bali is an island consisting of volcanoes, ricefields and temples.

This, of course, is an overstatement, yet one that has more than a grain of truth in it. Official Indonesian sources list over 10,000 registered shrines. This means that there are about two shrines per square kilometre. Adding to this the thousands of private shrines – and each Balinese house has a place specially reserved for the *songgah* (house temple) – we arrive at a staggering figure. Even more surprising is the fact that many shrines of this type are built of material requiring considerable technical skill and workmanship, and most of them are decorated with exquisite reliefs and sculptures.

The multitude of sacred buildings is a natural consequence of the social structure and of Balinese religious doctrines. With these is closely

Pura Tegeh Koripan, a temple uncannily close to the giant caldera rim of Batur, rides in clouds, smitten by icy gusts of wind. This split gate literally opens up to heaven. But from here, if Batur becomes active, one looks down into hell.

Above: The 'Moon of Pejeng' is housed in a pavilion in the ancient royal pura of Panataran Sasih Intaran, and only a section of its huge resonating disc is visible.

Right: The split gate of Pura Batur reveals this temple's principal gate, Padu Raksa. The steps and courtyard are covered with volcanic gravel.

linked the cult of the deceased and the ancestors. Furthermore, there are remnants of an ancient pre-Buddhist and pre-Hindu animism which in Bali coexist with the great religious beliefs imported from continental Asia. This animism survives to our day. It is almost omnipresent, surrounding everybody from his earliest years, permeating almost every aspect of Balinese existence – whether this applies to family life or daily work, the shared intimacy of Balinese homes, or life in the field and forest. Its magic hold is revealed at sunrise and sunset, on moonlit nights and with the approach of dawn, during the eclipse of the sun or moon. It is manifestly present in each rock and stone, in every tree, in the volcanoes, in the sea, in the springs, streams and rivers.

Water, that miraculous, life-giving element, played a role of special significance from the earliest days of animist imagery, as it did in subsequent Hinduism. Significantly, the earliest places of worship include *pura bejis* (temples of the holy spring) and *subak* temples. These sanctuaries differ in appearance. The simplest are merely a group of rocks or boulders surrounded by ancient trees, or caves containing a holy spring. Elsewhere, the fine, fully-developed structure of a *subak* temple is built in the middle of a lake or at the confluence of rivers, as befits Hindu notions of locations of great sanctity. A certain modesty in architectural conception characterizes all these temples, as does their exceptionally beautiful setting.

The sacral buildings, called *puras*, differ in significance and in function, but the inner design and architecture of these sanctuaries is, apart from minor exceptions, almost identical. The *pura* consists of three, or sometimes only two, walled-in enclosures, interconnected by gates, each enclosure forming a kind of court. Access to the first court is through the split gate. The second court is entered through a roofed-over gateway, which commonly is the temple's most beautiful structure. The last gateway leads to the third court – the sanctuary proper.

The first courtyard is a kind of vestibule usually comprising the kitchen and tables for the preparation of sacrificial offerings, the granaries and several *balés* – resting places for pilgrims. The *balé* is an elevated platform roofed over by a grass-covered structure, supported by pillars. The second courtyard usually contains the great *balé agung* – the place of assembly for the elders of the community. Another *balé* is used for the storage of *gamelan* instruments, different receptacles for sacrificial offerings and a tower with *kulkuls* – signal drums summoning the community for divine services or for profane tasks.

The third courtyard may contain a small pavilion consecrated to the founder, the patron of the village, if it is a village *pura*. Here the *lontars,* or sacred books, are kept and protected, along with other objects of worship and, frequently, there is a lingga, or stone phallus, symbol of fertility.

Other shrines, richly sculpted, are crowned with a small stone throne. The thrones are provided for the deities who are believed to descend from time to time from their celestial heights to the world of men, to preside over the religious festivals.

The most important and sculpturally the most interesting throne is the *padmasana*, the lotus throne consecrated to the sun god Surya, or to Siwa, in some localities. Noting that Siwa's throne invariably stands with its back towards Gunung Agung, it is easy to arrive at an image which might have inspired the ancient builders' minds: the supreme deity, giving his imaginary audience, is surrounded by a halo – the eruption of the sacred volcano . . . a vision of the early Indian icon of Siwa.

No less impressive is the group of shrines known as *merus*. They are

structures of timber erected on stone bases and possessing a varying number of small roofs of receding size. They are symbolic of the cosmic mountain, Mahameru, the dwelling place of the gods. The number of roofs (from three to eleven, but always an uneven number) indicates the deities' positions in the Balinese pantheon. Thus the *meru* consecrated to Siwa has eleven roofs, while the sanctuaries consecrated to Brahma and Wisnu have nine roofs. The highest roof protects the magically charged offering, a covered container holding nine precious stones or nine *pripihs* – tablets made of different metals with magic formulas inscribed upon them.

The ever-present silhouettes of the split gate and *meru*, hallmarks of Balinese architecture set into the landscape for the glory of the gods, became as well pointers to the originality of Balinese artistic achievements.

An outstanding memorial to the island's early history, and evidence of the process of Javanization undergone by Bali in the distant past, are the royal tombs of Tampaksiring dating from the eleventh century. The nine tombs, reflecting Hindu-Javanese prototypes, are hewn into the overhanging rocky walls flanking the narrow valley of the sacred Pakerisan River. They document the adoption of Javanese architectural styles of the day as well as that of earlier Indian models. The majestic tombs and the peaceful surrounding countryside evoke an unforgettable impression of solemnity.

The Goa Gajah (Elephant Cave) sanctuary near Budulu (Gianyar), also dating from the eleventh century, has a finely decorated bathing-place. For more than a thousand years, 'heavenly water-nymphs', sculpted in stone, have been pouring thin streams of water into the rectangular pool for the glory of the gods and the purification of man. The head of a giant demon protruding from the nearby rock guards the entrance to a small cell, a rocky hermitage. Siwaite monks dwelt here in the past.

Here in stone and rock, resisting the onslaught of centuries, are preserved two creative approaches. In their dignified static portrayal, the gargoyle nymphs are almost exact copies of east Javanese sculptures. The simple and well-proportioned architecture of the pool has a distinctly Javanese flavour. On the other hand, the sculptural decoration of the entrance to the hermitage is recognizably more Balinese. The lively bustle of the diminutive figures surrounding the central motif of the demon's head and the mesmerizing effect of his gaze are features that seem to foreshadow the rise of Balinese architecture of a later date, with its elaborate décor and dynamic style.

The full moon drifting through space above the centre of the universe, over the Mahameru mountain (Gunung Agung), every year for countless centuries has been followed with excitement and gratitude by thousands.

Gunung Agung is considered by the Balinese to be the centre of the world, a world given to him by his supreme god to whom he owes a debt of reverence and gratitude. A Balinese responds to this wondrous gift by work, prayer and sacrifice. And there is no better opportunity for this than at Pura Besakih, the island's most extensive temple territory, on the southwestern slope of the giant mountain.

Every year, at the time of the full moon of the fourth month of the Balinese calendar, endless processions from all parts of the island converge, bringing the people closer to their gods to receive their blessing. This is the night of one of the most splendid of mysteries; it has many names, and one of them is 'art'.

Besakih is not a single temple, but a group of three – the actual Pura Panataran Agung Besakih is in the centre; to the west lies Batu Madeg

Offerings pile up (above), as the procession (right) continues to flow into Pura Puseh, Desa Sempidi, near the holy spring of Sempidi. Stacks of offerings, veils of incense, walls of blossoms, never-ending processions of meticulously dressed and made-up women and girls, countless rites and performances, kulkul drums and gamelan music are all inexplicably stage-directed into a perfect harmony.

Pura Danu Bratan. This pura's meru with its eleven roofs symbolizes the Hindu notion of the cosmic mountain Mahameru, floating on the primeval ocean. This mountain, the centre of the universe, is not only known in Hindu cosmology, but also in Buddhist cosmology, and the Buddhists introduced this symbol as far east as China and Japan. Here on holy Lake Bratan, the Hindu shrine stands facing a Buddhistic stupa.

and to the east lies Dangin Kreteg. Pura Panataran Agung, 300 by 600 metres in size, is Bali's largest temple.

The present-day appearance of Besakih derives from the fourteenth century, but an inscription dating from 1007 proves that in the eleventh century it was a Buddhist sanctuary. And the differences in ritual, the Balinese rather than Hindu names of some of the deities and, finally, the actual topography of the temple seem to suggest that Besakih was a pre-Hindu terraced sanctuary, consecrated to the cult of the 'Master of the Mountain'.[4]

In contrast to other Balinese temples, the architecture is remarkably austere, its terraced starkness enhanced by the impressive background formed by the mountain. Here, as always, the Balinese builder showed his sense of harmony and proportion, his awareness of the spirit of the countryside. Indeed, perhaps it was the spirit of the countryside, its physical manifestations (eruptions, lava flows, tectonic disturbances) that taught the Balinese, those masters in coexistence with death, to build these light, almost 'mobile' edifices that can always be renewed.

On numerous occasions, Besakih has experienced the rage of its gods (and not only Besakih – in 1916-17 alone, volcanic eruptions destroyed 2,341 sanctuaries). And yet Besakih remains the worshipped and revered 'maternal temple' of Bali. The eruption of Gunung Agung in 1963

The main façade of the Pura Dalem of Jagaraga. This pura is an example of sculptural efflorescence typical of the north coast of Bali. Here the sanctuaries are overcharged with a truly demonic energy. Every sculpture, down to its last seemingly insignificant detail, appears to be in flux; there is no space left to relax, to contemplate. The contrast with the architecture of central and southern Bali is striking.

destroyed several villages, about 2000 people perished and almost 300,000 lost their homes. In spite of this the mountain remains the symbolic centre of the universe, home of the trinity made nearly manifest by the glorious altar with three thrones consecrated to Siwa, Wisnu and Brahma. Once in the Balinese year, the gods will descend from the mountain, the centre of the universe, to assume, invisibly, their places on the thrones.

Batur – to use a layman's description – is a volcano within a volcano.[5] The outer crater's rim forms a cauldron which in the course of past millennia has been filled again and again by the inner crater; lava, that elixir of life and death, is magically transformed into fertile soil.

Batur not only shapes the surrounding countryside, but also, to a large extent, has dictated the activities of the people who through the ages have defied its constant threat.

Batur is one of the most mysterious places in Bali – a gateway giving access to the living past of the island's people, a territorial circle enclosing their routine lives, which, in a split second, can become tragic.

At the fringe of the outer crater, which is one of the world's biggest natural amphitheatres (over forty kilometres in circumference), stands Pura Batur, a solitary temple at the height of 1,200 metres above sea level. The appearance of the temple is always changing, being subjected to

mercurial changes of weather and never-ending transformations of light. These affect not only Pura Batur, but the entire scenery inside the crater. The large, crescent-shaped lake glittering at the cauldron's bottom, between outer rim and cone-shaped centre, is fittingly described as the 'colour-changing lake'.

Pura Batur is a spacious temple, possessing tall, majestic gates with incomplete sculptural decoration. The courtyard, full of different *balés*, gods' thrones and *candis*, is covered with a thick layer of black volcanic ash. Mixed into the ashes, some Chinese coins are testimonials to bygone ancient prayers and sacrifices.

Here, the quietude of a sacred place delineates the boundary between annihilation and life. Such a setting is bound to transform any religious ritual into a transcendent spectacle in which art, dance, music and the illusionistic ambience of the temple and its surroundings all play their part.

The term 'art', as used here, applies not just to fine arts, including sculpture and relief ornamentation which form an integral part of temple architecture; it also includes smaller, mobile artefacts, such as different sacramental instruments, jewellery and other objects of personal adornment, and exquisite garments always made of precious cloth; and it embraces all manner of sacrificial offerings, frequently supplemented by delicate minor objects, masks, ceramics, lamps and the like.

Many of the rites performed here reflect mythological notions of the universe and of man's position in the cosmos. These conceptions are projected into the architecture, as in Pura Batur's orientation, which is determined by the temple's celestial bearings and the volcano's dominating position. The view of the peak of Gunung Batur, seen through the temple gates, has an astronomical and astrological significance.

One of the loneliest places in Bali is the village of Trunyan near the eastern bank of Batur Lake. Although Trunyan can be reached in less than an hour by motor boat from the opposite bank, the village sees few visitors. The only access is by crossing the lake; there are no other routes, since to climb down the steep slopes of the inner wall of the crater, overgrown by impenetrable tropical vegetation and in many places dropping down in vertical cliffs straight into the lake, would be impossible. And so, the village of Trunyan, with a few dozen inhabitants, became, without any official designation, of its own accord as it were, a reservation for the original inhabitants of Bali, known as *Bali-aga*.

Here the sound of the outer world is but a faint echo dimmed by the village's inaccessibility and by codes sanctioning different customs and modes of life, and preventing the integration of the *Bali-aga* with the rest of the population. Here, more of the pre-Hindu heritage has been preserved than elsewhere in Bali and the Hindu elements that have taken hold here have undergone a complicated metamorphosis.

The village comprises a few buildings and a *pura* crouching in the shade of a magnificent *waringin*, that sacred fig-tree which has remained unaffected by the passage of centuries, and even by the eruptions of the volcanic mountain towering on the opposite bank of the lake ten kilometres away from Trunyan.

The village and its *pura* conceal a few surprising features. Some of the buildings look almost as if they have been transferred from Tibet, once the domain of northern Buddhism. Certain elements of other buildings are vaguely reminiscent of certain elements of Japanese architecture. How did these affinities come about? The *pura* contains one of the biggest *balé agungs* in Bali. Why? one wonders, considering the small population of the village. The tallest building of the *pura* – the *meru dalem sakti* – houses

the biggest stone statue in Bali, portraying Ratu Gedé Pantcering Jagat, god of the netherworld. The statue, almost four metres in height, is hidden throughout the year in this *meru*. On a special day, the statue is painted white and coated with sugar-water and honey – perhaps to gain the favour of this god who is honoured as the protector and guardian of the village.

Barong berutuk, the ancient dance which still forms part of important festivals at Trunyan, is remarkable for the use of primitive masks, crude by Balinese standards. The dancers wear garments consisting of the foliage of trees held to be sacred. The overall impression is reminiscent of some masks of Pacific provenance. Is this mere chance or surviving evidence of ancient contacts?

Can a satisfactory answer ever be provided to these questions?

About 200 metres away from the village, behind a cliff dropping down into the lake, is the burial place. Following an ancient ritual, the deceased are neither interred nor cremated, as is the general practice in Bali, but placed on low bamboo trestles, provided with the barest necessities of daily life and left to their natural transformation.

Numerous strange practices – divination, exorcism, astrology and the elaborate religious rituals – are indications that the *Bali-aga* of Trunyan still cling to their ancient past, barely gilded with a crust of Hinduism.

Bali is often described as an island of abundance and contrast. This refers to the scenery, to the workings of nature which on so small a territory has produced such an amazingly rich variety of life. The same is true of Balinese art and architecture, which abound in contrasts and display such tropical exuberance. A few examples may illustrate the point.

Equatorially, Bali is in its whole length divided into two parts by a range of mountains reaching as high as 3,142 metres. There are numerous lakes. Bratan, the lake in the crater of the volcano of the same name, is known as the 'holy mountain lake' and considered to have all the attributes of holiness – such as the miraculous healing powers of its water, and the amazing fertility of the fields irrigated by its waters. On the southern bank of this beautiful lake, on a small islet, stands Danu Bratan, one of the oldest temples in the province of Buleleng. The position and appearance of the temple (comprising only two *merus*) are not incidental, for they symbolize the cosmos. Ancient Buddhist and Hindu mythology visualizes the universe as composed of soaring mountain ranges encompassing the oceans of the world with Mahameru mountain emerging from the centre. The temple of Danu Bratan evokes this ancient vision: it represents the centre of the world, surrounded by the primeval oceans which are the waters of the lake, framed by a mountain range – the walls of Bratan crater. The symbolic imagery conveyed by this small sanctuary reflects its paramount importance as the centre of uranic divine services and the meeting place for the members of most of the *subaks* of the region. The modern beauty of Danu Bratan is an exemplary embodiment of the canonically prescribed laws on proportions recorded in the ancient Indian writings known as *Silpa Shastra.*

In complete contrast to buildings of this type are the *puras* on the coast of northern Bali. While the appeal of Danu Bratan lies in its simplicity and perfect fusion with the surrounding landscape, the style of most northern coastal temple architecture is characterized by a more elaborate planning of the temple grounds and a complexity of artistic embellishment which is sheerly overwhelming. Here, it seems that the surrounding scenery was not taken into consideration when a site was chosen for the temple buildings. This is in direct contrast to the premeditated choice of sites in other parts of Bali.

Masks of Barong (left) and Rangda (below) the protagonists of the best known of all the Balinese performances. The shadow-puppet of Rangda (above), of c. 1900, has all the magic properties of the Rangda mask.

Another difference between the south and the north concerns the building materials used. In the southern and central parts of Bali, the most frequently used material besides timber is brick and light grey sandstone (walls – brick; ornamentation – sandstone; or, less frequently, only one type of building material is used). In contrast, most *puras* in northern Bali are built of dark, sometimes even black, soft sandstone. Tuff, volcanic rock, is occasionally used as an additional building material in both regions, but its use is nearly always restricted to free-standing sculptures.

Although a detailed description of northern Balinese shrines and sanctuaries would require many more pages, the following is an attempt to describe some of their artistic and spiritual aspects.

The most striking feature of practically all these buildings is their lush ornamentation and the multitude of sculpted figures, giving the impression that the builders never had enough available space to cram in all their visions. Hence, the unrestrained adding on of hundreds of consoles, cornices and mouldings.

The chief structural components of northern Balinese architecture are surface relief, bas-relief (often combined with true sculpture) and sometimes flat engravings of the surface, bordering on etching. The Balinese know how to make the most of the different qualities of materials used and their texture. The sculptor-carvers use their techniques with consummate mastery when creating free-standing statuary.

The great majority of such *puras* are the *pura dalems*, temples associated with chthonic cults. This accounts for the profusion of different underworld deities, gods and godlings, demons or merely the symbols of these deities in these *puras*. The recurrence of erotic motifs is also symptomatic of the northern areas, being almost non-existent elsewhere in Bali.

To sum up, the *puras* of northern Bali are characterized by a tendency to elaborate architectural solutions to their limitations. The fusion of decorative adornment and infernal themes frequently produces a visually powerful effect. Obviously, this was the intention of the builders and one is bound to admit that their effort was not in vain. Entering any of these vestibules leading to the underworld is an artistic experience radically different from that gained by entering Danu Bratan. While at Bratan art gives substance to contemplation, here in the north it assumes the form of a memento mori.

The *pura dalem*, or temple of death, ranks alongside the *pura beji* and the *subak* temple as one of the earliest types of sacral architecture. Here the influence of Hinduism is significant as, for example, in the *pura dalem* called Durga Kutri Desa, near the village of Blahbatuh, which dates from the eleventh century. The statue of Durga, the goddess of death, is almost purely Indian.

The *pura dalem* is usually situated in the *kelod*, or towards the sea, part of a village. It is sometimes also found in desolate places set aside for cremation burial. Cremation does not take place immediately after death, but the deceased is interred for a varying period of time, before the priest, following the ritual code, specifies a suitable cremation date. The body is then exhumed and burnt ceremoniously on a funeral pyre. There are individual, but also collective cremations, and they differ from place to place.

The death temple, a sanctuary of gloomy appearance, which the Balinese avoids entering except on festive occasions, becomes at the time of cremations and posthumous rites the scene of colourful and exciting events full of suspense and drama. The faces of the relatives and other actors in this protracted ritual mirror expectation, tension, but also relief and a kind of blissful contentment, because the flames open the way

Above: A huge demon's head keeps guard over the entrance to an ancient hermit's cave, Goa Gajah, dating from the eleventh century. Here, the demonic, frightening aspect is, in typical Balinese fashion, juxtaposed with the playful.

Opposite, above: Just before a soul is released, the sarcophagus collapsing into the flames reveals the bones and ashes. These will be collected and thrown into the sea after various purification ceremonies.

Opposite, below: The Barong Kat. The 'Kakekom', a Balinese poem, relates how Siwa sent his aide to earth as Barong to eat the offerings left at Galungan. But a widow from Jirah in eastern Java, a powerful black magician called Rangda, interfered. She asked and got permission from the goddess Durga to kill the Barong. A terrible fight ensued in which Barong was killed, only to be promptly brought to life again by Siwa. All Balinese masks used in dramas are sanctified by offerings at their creation and before and often after every performance in which they partake. They receive the reverential treatment due to supernatural beings.

Top: This offering, called gebogan, is carved in the shape of a beautiful female wearing the elaborate hairdo of a dancer. The pyramid of fruits and ricecakes is built up on a wooden support, the central part of which represents the dancer's skirt and sash. Combining seemingly incongruous elements in such a fanciful way is typically Balinese.

Above: Erotic illustration from a Balinese book, engraved into the leaves of the lontar palm. After being engraved, the leaves were rubbed with soot and oil which stuck only in the engraved grooves. The leaves, cut into long strips of equal size, were then perforated and bound between two wooden panels.

to reincarnation. The almost theatrical effect of such cremations is dramatized by the contrast between the deep green twilight of the forest and the blaze of dozens of funeral pyres. Crowds of people, dressed in ceremonial garments, are by turns illuminated by the leaping flames and hidden in clouds of blue smoke, and the roar of the fire burning the pyres blends with the sound of *gamelan* music, all creating a performance worthy of the best masters of stage design. Here the fine sense of contrast and dramatic effect – so natural to the Balinese – comes to the fore. This is scenography in a truly grand style.

To watch Balinese dances is to enter a world of ancient religious lore, epic poetry, drama and music, a world of shapes, colours and lights, of unparalleled beauty and fascination. It is to enter a totally different, unexplored territory of the visual arts. The Barong Rangda is the most popular mimic dance of all. Leaving aside the symbolic and ethical message of the Barong/Rangda, which has already been discussed, let us concentrate on the visually most prominent aspect of the dance – the masks. The masks, especially those worn by the two central protagonists – Barong and Rangda, often seen as embodiments of good and evil[6] – have an almost hypnotic effect. The moment they appear, the audience is gripped with excitement bordering on fear. It would be difficult to find (with the exception perhaps of the sacred *tsam* dance of Tibet and the Japanese *kyogen*, both ancient Buddhist temple dances) counterpart examples in the theatre of other nations, producing a similarly powerful effect. Although much of the fascination stems from the scenography of the Barong/Rangda performance, it seems that the decisive factor here is the actual workmanship of the artist who made these masks, the sculptural value of the masks themselves.

Sculpture, regardless of the material used, is the dominant medium of expression in Balinese fine arts. The extraordinary appeal of Balinese sculpture should perhaps be sought in the wealth of inspirational stimuli. The profusion of outside influences provided the breeding ground for the development of Balinese art and of Balinese sculpture in particular.

Here are two examples suggesting possible sources of inspiration for the masks of the Rangda and the Barong, masks which, for the Balinese, possess a significance reaching far beyond their actual role in the drama.

The physical appearance of Rangda, the sorceress, the queen of black magic, is so unique that one tends to reject the idea that this monster might have been created by man. Looking for an inspiration for the Rangda mask in nature, an interesting possibility is that its origin may lie not in Bali, but in islands lying 500 kilometres north east of Bali.[7] This would suggest the existence of possible Balinese contacts with distant islands. The model in question is the skull of the *babirusa*, a pig-like animal native to Sulawesi.

The face of Barong, that mysterious creature of a somewhat strange leonine appearance, has its prototype in the lion of early Indian Buddhist sculpture dating from the first centuries AD. In China, a similar lion symbolizes strength and resilience (the symbol first occurs during the Tang Dynasty, AD 618–907, and in Vietnam and Japan as well, a leonine mask is still a standard feature of theatre performances and New Year processions).

This is not the place for a detailed description of the shadow-play theatre, its scope, scale and significance. Our concern here is with some of its visual aspects, as they have a close bearing on Balinese drawing and painting.

Up to the beginning of the twentieth century the *wayang* shadow-play

This stone sculpture, a female head resting in the palm of the male above her, is unique in its execution and in its symbolic implications. The huge stone block, measuring almost a metre and a half in height, is divided into two equal parts. These, barely touching, give the impression of the massive man's head hovering in permanent suspension over the woman's head. They may be Satyawati and Salya, known from the Balinese version of the 'Bharatayudha'. In the famous love scene, Satyawati, afraid her lover is about to meet his death, twists his loincloth around them both, to prevent him from leaving her. To no avail – her premonition comes true and she takes her own life. The stone has been imbued with life, and nature has joined forces with art. The creeper following the sculpted lines embellishes the lovers with splashes of green, the colour of vitality.

theatre took the place of drawing, then almost non-existent in Bali. This type of puppet-show leaves no room for doubt that the substitute for drawing was, in effect, a living medium. It is very likely that, because of this alive quality, no need arose in Bali for drawing of the type customary in China, Vietnam and Japan, where graphic art developed into book illustration, calligraphy, New Year prints, prints serving theatrical and other purposes, and, finally, into separate graphic sheets, a variety typical of Japanese art of the past few centuries.

The bulk of Balinese graphic art comprises drawings (or rather engravings) of miniature size. These were cut into leaves of *lontar* palms, which were then bound into volumes. The influence of *wayang* was so strong that the artist, in most illustrations, actually portrayed puppets. Hence they are described as illustrations in '*wayang* style'.

Equally, discounting twentieth-century painting, Balinese painting has a distinctively stiff and angular *wayang*-like style. Traditionally Balinese painting finds its main application in the decoration of long draperies in *puras* depicting various mythological scenes, and in large-surface astrological calendars.

Above: The lotus throne with seats for Siwa, Brahma and Wisnu. It rests on the world turtle, Bedawang 'Nala, who is entwined by snakes. Monarchic temple, Pura Kehen, Bangli.

Right: Small and modest, a meru symbolizing the cosmic mountain, against the majestic backdrop of Gunung Batur – Balinese relativity.

Although *wayang* has retained its appeal as a beloved and instructive show, good *dalangs* (puppeteers – frequently also puppet-makers) are rapidly decreasing in number and so Balinese puppets have become collectors' items, gradually finding their way into museum showcases and private art collections.

The capacity of a Balinese to perceive life as a great theatrical spectacle in which he is both viewer and actor gives him the opportunity to direct the dramaturgy and stage design of his entire existence.

Therefore, any celebration – and they are countless, for the Balinese love to perform their ambiguous actor/spectator roles – always means a dazzling artistic performance. Everything that a Balinese believes in, everything that he does, everything that he lives for, he projects into festivals and processions. The manner in which this is accomplished can justly be described as genuine choreography.

Perhaps the most stunning example of a festival in which different aspects of the Balinese artistic genius are combined is the great ten-day festival of Galungan. Over ten-metre long bamboo poles, or *penjors*, are placed in front of every house, however small, and from the *penjors* are hung offerings of unhusked rice and flowers, gifts to the gods, symbols of gratitude for the harvest, and for general prosperity. People wear their most exquisite ceremonial garments and their most glittering jewellery, and day after day processions, dances and dramatic performances take place.

The *odalans*, or festivals honouring the anniversaries of individual shrines, last for three days. Women go in procession to the *puras*, bearing offerings of fruit, rice-cakes and flowers which are decorated with many minor gems of folk art, such as minute masks and tiny ceramic objects.

There are also ceremonies in honour of mountains, volcanoes, lakes, rivers, and a whole range of natural phenomena, including sacred trees, flowers and their divine patrons. A good example of a festival of this type is Tumpek Uduh, during which offerings are made to gardens, fruit trees and palm trees. Here, offerings mostly consist of holy water, handfuls of seeds or fruit, flowers and great numbers of incense sticks; the ash of these, carefully collected, is returned to the earth.

There are various agricultural festivals, some of which have already been described earlier, and daily offerings are made to Dewi Sri at altars standing right in the middle of ricefields.

The artistic sphere, too, affords abundant opportunities for feasts and festivals. Special days and holidays commemorate the patrons of different arts and crafts – swordsmiths, goldsmiths and other craftsmen uniting to produce sacred *krises* and different sacramental instruments. A special festival is consecrated to Dewi Saraswati, the beautiful goddess of learning, literature and art. To her, homage is paid in recognition of the gift of learning she bestows on man. The muses of astronomy, astrology, drama, dance and music have their own festival days, too.

The festivals of Bali are a shining display of arts and crafts of all domains and dimensions, of all colours and fragrances. They are the essence of Balinese life. Most of these festivals are unthinkable without processions, pilgrimages, purification ceremonies and sacrificial offerings. It is no exaggeration to claim that the very act of making a sacrificial offering is an art in its own right. The perfection of the gestures, comparable to the refinement of those of the Japanese tea ceremony, the elements of pantomime and, finally, the sacrifice itself, with which the Balinese identifies with such emotional intensity and fervour that he feels himself to be the sacrificial offering – all these events, set against a natural scenic background and supplemented by numerous artefacts, constitute an art of consonance.

NOTES

These notes are not meant as a scholarly apparatus, but rather to indicate to the reader what sources have been used, and also to guide him in the direction of books and articles which may be of interest. In the cases where articles are listed by title in the *Bibliography*, only the title of the article is mentioned; in those cases where the articles are found in books which are listed in the *Bibliography*, both article and book are mentioned in the *Notes*. For the sake of brevity, in some cases only authors and dates are given, or only author, if there is only one book or article by him in the *Bibliography*. All studies reprinted in *Bali Studies in Life, Thought and Ritual* and *Bali: Further Studies in Life, Thought and Ritual* have been translated from Dutch into English.

THE ANCESTORS

1 There are many versions of the creation myth (as of everything) in Bali. The following summary is based mainly on original Balinese sources, translated and published by Hooykaas in 1973 and 1974. Other versions have been translated by Soebadio, and one is quoted in Belo's 'The Balinese Temper' (1935; reprinted in her *Traditional Balinese Culture*) one in McPhee's 'The Balinese Wajang Koelit' and one in Covarrubias's *Island of Bali*.

2 'It may be well known to the reader', Stutterheim wrote in 1931, in his article, 'The Meaning of the Hindu-Javanese Candi', 'that among the Indonesian people a tendency is found to place the land of the souls in an uninhabited and inaccessible country. For the inhabitants of small islands it is situated in the feared and unknown neighbour islands. On islands without mountains it lies in barren and uninhabited plains. On mountainous islands, however, it is placed on the mountains. It must have been so before, and is still partly so in Java and Bali.'

3 Regarding this, see, for instance, Swellengrebel's 'Introduction' to *Bali: Studies in Life, Thought and Ritual*.

4 Some of this archaic world can still be recalled, thanks to a fascinating photographic reconstruction made by Goris and Dronkers in the first chapters of their *Bali: Atlas Kebudajaan*.

5 This report is quoted in *The History of the Liang Dynasty*.

6 Swellengrebel, *op. cit.*

7 A great deal of this tradition is preserved in *Usana Bali* (discussed in Friederich, *De Oesana Bali*, 1847), *Usana Jawa* and *Kidoeng Pamantjangah* (edited by Berg, 1927 and 1929).

8 Vlekke, *Nusantara: A History of Indonesia*.

9 De Klerck, *History of the Netherlands East Indies*.

10 Hanna, in *Bali Profile*, summarizes the first European contacts. Already eighty years before Houtman's ships arrived at Bali's shores, Magellan might have spotted the island, but we have no record of him stopping there. This is the case also with other possible visitors – Portuguese sailors in the mid-sixteenth century, Sir Francis Drake and perhaps Thomas Cavendish. Their meetings with Bali, of whatever character they might have been, left no visible traces either on Bali or on the European view of the island.

11 See de Klerck, *op. cit.*

12 Again, there are several accounts of this event, which differ in detail and point of view. This one is from Hanna's *Bali Profile*. Balinese descriptions have been collected and summarized by Mishra in 1973 and 1976; a Dutch eyewitness report was written by H. M. van Weede in 1908; Covarrubias describes it eloquently; and a fictionalized account was given in *A Tale from Bali* by Baum.

13 According to Worsley in *Babad Buleleng*, state histories were mostly read in state temples, but also, in Boon's words, 'Houseyards that aspire to high rank often record a version of their own history to be read on festive occasions in the ancestor temple . . .' (*The Anthropological Romance of Bali, 1597-1972*).

14 Grader, 'The State Temples of Mengwi' (1949), reprinted in *Bali: Studies in Life, Thought and Ritual*.

15 See Grader, 'Pura Meduwe Karang at Kubutambahan' (1940), reprinted in *Bali: Further Studies in Life, Thought and Ritual*.

THE HEIRS

1 Covarrubias, *Island of Bali*.

2 The *Desa-monografiën*, written by the Dutch civil servant and scholar, F. A. Liefrinck during the 1880s, are still considered a valuable basis for more recent studies, like those of Grader, I Gusti Gde Raka, and Birkelbach. All of them testify to the superb organization and achievement of the Balinese.

3 According to Birkelbach's 'The *Subak* Association' *subak* literally means 'joining waters'. Grader, in his 1939 study of the irrigation system in Jembrana (reprinted in *Bali: Studies in Life, Thought and Ritual*), gives the legal definition as 'a group of *sawahs* (ricefields) which, being watered from the same conduit or the same branch of a conduit, forms an irrigation association,' though he points out that there are exceptions to this.

4 The *subak*, as Geertz, for instance, has shown in 'The Wet and the Dry', is in no sense a collective farm. Each peasant family owns its land and consumes or sells its own products, after what is due to the *subak* has been deducted.

5 Geertz, 'Tihingan: A Balinese Village'.

6 Geertz, 'Person, Time and Conduct in Bali' (1966); reprinted in his *The Interpretation of Cultures*.

7 There are many rules applying to what people of different castes might or might not do. For example, in classical Bali only the 'twice born', or higher castes, were allowed to wear *krises* with golden or ivory hilts, while Sudras had to be content with wooden hilts.

8 This is made clear by figures from Birkelbach, *op. cit.*

9 See Geertz's article on the village of Tihingan.

10 See Geertz, *ibid.*

11 Kersten, *Bali* (trans. Boon in *The Anthropological Romance of Bali, 1597-1972*.).

12 Bateson and Mead, *Balinese Character*. McPhee, Geertz and Belo have noted the same thing, from different points of view.

13 Bateson, 'Bali: The Value System of a Steady State'.

14 Belo, 'A Study of a Balinese Family'.

15 Geertz, 'Person, Time and Conduct in Bali'. Mead makes the same point in her 1955 article on children and ritual in Bali, reprinted in Belo, ed., *Traditional Balinese Culture*.

16 Geertz, *ibid.*

17 In some villages, as Bateson and Mead observed in *Balinese Character*, the birth of a great-grandchild terminates a man's citizenship, and if he meets his great-grandchild, he is supposed to give him a present before speaking to him.

18 Geertz, 'Person, Time and Conduct in Bali'.

19 Bateson and Mead, *op. cit.*

20 Jane Belo, who spent many years in Bali during the 1930s studying the culture, says, in *Trance in Bali*, '*Paling*, they say, is not to know where the north is'; Clifford Geertz describes *paling* thus in his 1972 study of a Balinese cockfight (reprinted in his *The Interpretation of Cultures*): '. . . special vertigo, the dizzy, disoriented, lost, turned around feeling one gets when one's place in . . . the coordinates of social space is not clear . . . is a tremendously disfavored, immensely anxiety producing state. The Balinese regard the exact maintenance of spatial orientation (not to know where the north is is to be crazy), balance, decorum, status relationship and so forth as fundamental to ordered life . . .'

THE GODS

1 Hooykaas, *Religion in Bali*.

2 See Grader's article on Pemayun Temple (1939), reprinted in *Bali: Studies in Life, Thought and Ritual*.

3 This is according to Covarrubias in *Island of Bali*.

4 Goris, 'The Temple System' (1938) reprinted in *Bali: Studies in Life, Thought and Ritual*.

5 Grader, in 'The State Temples of Mengwi' (1949), reprinted in *Bali: Studies in Life, Thought and Ritual*.

6 Liefrinck, in *Bali en Lombok* (1927); part of this study was reprinted in *Bali: Further Studies in Life, Thought and Ritual*, as 'Rice Cultivation'.

7 Boon, *The Anthropological Romance of Bali, 1597-1972*.

8 See, for instance, Jane Belo's *Bali*. Boon too (*op. cit.*) says, 'in some respects the ancestor temple represents the ideal unity of its congregation.'

9 This is according to Hooykaas's *Religion in Bali*.

10 In the view of some scholars, the *sungguhu* may be a remnant of a former Wisnu sect in Bali. Another anachronistic distinction is between the *pedanda Siwa* and the *pedanda Boda*, the latter being connected with ancient Balinese Buddhism. Today, *pedandas Boda* are distinguished by their short hair, and flowers worn behind both ears. According to Korn and others, these not very numerous priests in fact consider Siwa to be the highest god, as do the *pedandas Siwa*. Since, in Bali, the popular

belief is that Buddha is a younger brother of Siwa, the Balinese do not make much distinction between these two, and invite to their ceremonies whichever one happens to be more accessible (usually the *pedanda Siwa*); if they are rich enough, they may invite both priests to officiate together.

11 Belo, *Trance in Bali*.

12 Belo, *ibid*.

13 See, for instance, Grader's article on Pura Meduwe Karang (1940), reprinted in *Bali: Further Studies in Life, Thought and Ritual*.

14 Quoted in Mershon's article, 'Five Great Elements: *Pancha Maha Buta*', in Belo, ed., *Traditional Balinese Culture*.

15 Goris, 'The Temple System' (1938), reprinted in *Bali: Studies in Life, Thought and Ritual*.

16 Like Rangda, like Barong, like the banyan tree, which is both a shelter and a threat, like the split gate, which is both frightening and a way to heaven, the *pura puseh* and *pura dalem* are not simply 'good' and 'evil'. The tension between the two extremes, *kaja* and *kelod*, divine and demonic, is manifested most clearly in the *pura balé agung*, but it is also present in both of the other temples. There are abodes for the celestial deities in the *pura dalem*, and there are demons present in the *pura puseh* too. In many villages assemblies are convened on certain occasions in the *pura dalem*.

17 Boon, *op. cit*.

18 I will never forget the minutes, several years ago, that I spent on the sloppy, steep path a metre or so wide, leading from the Tanah Lot temple in southern Bali, with a sheer drop to the sea reefs about ten metres below. It was at the time of an *odalan*, one of the most popular in Bali. Those who had finished their prayers pushed their way down, hundreds if not thousands of them. Those who were arriving streamed up, with huge offerings piled on their heads, babies in their arms. We moved inch by inch. Several times my unlucky left leg was suspended in the air above the sea, and I kept myself still among the living only by clutching at any stranger – man, woman, girl, boy – who was at my side at that moment. The slightest echo of panic would have resulted in diaster, but nobody (except me) was nervous.

19 See, for instance, Mershon's 'Five Great Elements: *Pancha Maha Buta*' and Hooykaas's *Cosmogony*.

THE RULERS

1 de Zoete and Spies, *Dance and Drama in Bali*.

2 Helms, L. V., *Pioneering in the Far East and Journeys to California in 1849 and to the White Sea in 1848*.

3 The legal aspect of ruler-peasant communal relations is described in detail by van Eck and Liefrinck in their *Kerta-Sima*. It has been convincingly argued that there was no absolute tyranny in Bali, particularly by Korn in his *Adatrecht*, and by many others since. Wittfogel, however, used Bali as an example for his 'oriental despotism' theories.

4 Often more than six temples are listed as making the *sadkahyangan*, the term being interpreted in different ways – and with different temples – by individual dynasties, rulers, and even provinces and princedoms. The one named virtually every time the *sadkahyangan* is mentioned is, of course, the all-Bali temple, Pura Besakih. The best studies on the topic are still Grader's (1949) on the state temples of Mengwi, reprinted in *Bali: Studies in Life, Thought and Ritual*, and Goris's on Pura Besakih (1948), reprinted in *Bali: Further Studies in Life, Thought and Ritual*.

5 Geertz, *Negara*.

6 Geertz, 'Politics Past, Politics Present', reprinted in *The Interpretation of Cultures*.

7 Mead, 'The Strolling Players in the Mountains of Bali' (1939), reprinted in Belo, ed., *Traditional Balinese Culture*.

8 In Geertz and Geertz, *Kinship in Bali* (1939), reprinted in Belo, ed., *Traditional Balinese Culture*.

9 In *Kinship in Bali*, Geertz and Geertz discuss this in detail.

10 Geertz, 'Politics Past, Politics Present'.

11 Panji Sakti, the founder of the Buleleng kingdom described in the *Babad Buleleng* was one such famous and successful Balinese upstart. The recent dramatic growth of the popularity of another, who lived in the seventeenth century, Jayaprana, is a subject of Franken's study on the festival of Jayaprana at Kalianget, reprinted in *Bali: Studies in Life, Thought and Ritual*.

12 Geertz, *Negara*.

13 In his comments on the Balinese royal view of war, Worsley writes: 'Indeed, one gains the impression that we are here [in the war between Buleleng and Mengwi] confronted not so much with a war as with a tournament in which both armies display their heroic qualities and skills in battle. Having established that both armies contained excellent men . . . and when the ruler of Mengwi has satisfied himself of the military prowess of the northern Balinese [i.e. his enemies], the battle was broken off, and both kings were joined in . . . brotherly love.'

14 Geertz, *Negara*.

THE TIME OF TRANCE

1 Covarrubias, *Island of Bali*.

2 Mead, 'Children and Ritual in Bali' (1955), reprinted in Belo, ed., *Traditional Balinese Culture*.

3 Belo, *Trance in Bali*. Jane Belo, with Walter Spies, in researching the different kind of *sanghyangs* practised in only one area, found there were twenty. Many of the trances described by Belo were reported to her by Spies, whose descriptions of animal trances remain, after fifty years, the best we have.

4 De Zoete and Spies, *Dance and Drama in Bali*.

5 De Zoete and Spies, *ibid*.

6 The Balinese enormously enjoy close physical contact in a crowd. Considerable cultural importance has been ascribed to the crowd, the bustle, *ramé*. There is, however, as far as I have seen, nothing even implicitly sexual in the *ramé* passion when trance is not involved. During *ramé* in the non-trance condition, the sexes are usually separated – only men fight for the cremation towers, for instance, and women place themselves in a separate part of the crowd during many ceremonies. When, during a ceremony, a young couple uses the opportunity to flirt, the pair leaves the crowd. Here the constrast is best manifested, perhaps, with the theatrically sexual behaviour shown during some forms of trance.

7 Belo, *Trance in Bali*.

8 Belo, *ibid*.

9 Bateson and Mead, *Balinese Character*.

10 Belo, *op. cit*.

11 It has been repeatedly pointed out by my Balinese informants that the threshold, not only in trance, but also in dance and drama, is of primary importance. Some informants spoke of the actors emerging into the limelight being gods and ancestors entering the human world. Others described the place beyond the limits of the scene, or a temple court during a trance, as being the unknown that 'cannot be named'. The split gate is often thought of as such a threshold, as well. It visibly tempts and threatens trancers, and when they dare to pass it, stimulates them into violent spasms of trance. 'The effect of an actor or dancer entering the stage is that of someone approaching from a great distance,' wrote Colin McPhee in his *Dance in Bali*. 'This entrance, this emergence into full visibility, is delayed as long as possible, as though the dancer could not bear to cross the magic line . . . The entrance dances, perhaps the most beautiful of all in their delay and abstract elegance, take a long time to perform.'

12 De Zoete and Spies, *Dance and Drama in Bali*.

13 For an example of this, see Bateson's 1937 study, 'An Old Temple and a New Myth' reprinted in Belo, ed., *Traditional Balinese Culture*.

14 Belo, *op. cit*. While trance has been an important vehicle of change in Bali, it is, of course, far from being the only one. I hope this book makes it clear that the Balinese established change as one of the fundamental positive values of their civilization. The very definition of *kelod*, the chthonic sphere, as not absolutely black and life-destroying, but as fertile and inspiring as well, has meant that change is always seen as ethically acceptable. Topographically and historically, to use one of many examples, a function rather similar to that of *kelod* has been carried out by a subculture of the northern provinces of the island, traditionally more exposed to the outside world than the south. The north Balinese mores, music, dance, architecture and social relations, generally less orthodox and more experimental, were always in contrast to the norm.

15 Mead, *Male and Female*.

THE IMAGES

1 Ramseyer, *The Art and Culture of Bali*.

2 Galestin, *Indonesie, Algemeen Kunstgescheidenis*.

3 This 'creation', completed in the 1970s on the southern coast of Australia, is the work of V. Christo.

4 Ramseyer, *op. cit*.

5 Actually, a double-coned crater formation, the outer cone of which is called 'caldera', the inner, 'somma'.

6 Our comment presents no more than a generalized account of the symbols. The actual relationship of two conflicting principles enacted in the Barong/Rangda performance receives different interpretations.

7 This assumption was brought to the author's attention by J. Winter, zoologist and artist.

BIBLIOGRAPHY

This bibliography gives only a fraction of the available literature on Bali, as it is concerned only with sources used in the preparation of the text, or referred to in the text. A few books, such as *Bali: Studies in Life, Thought, and Ritual*, contain several articles referred to in the text. These articles have been listed only in the notes, and only the title of the book in which they are to be found is included in the bibliography. In the case where only one or two articles are cited from a volume, the articles themselves are listed in the bibliography, followed by the titles of the books in which they appear. In the interests of economy of space, and of simplicity, the original sources for reprinted articles are not given. When an English translation of a Dutch or Indonesian source is available, only the translation is listed in the bibliography.

Bali: Studies in Life, Thought, and Ritual, ed. W. F.Wertheim and others, W. van Hoeve, The Hague and Bandung (1960).

Bali: Further Studies in Life, Thought, and Ritual, ed. J. van Baal and others, W. van Hoeve, The Hague and Bandung (1969).

Bateson, G., 'Bali: The Value System of a Steady State', in *Social Structure: Studies Presented to A. R. Radcliffe-Brown*, ed. Meyer Fortes, Russell and Russell, New York (1963): 35–53.

Bateson, G. and Mead, M., *Balinese Character*, New York Academy of Sciences, New York (1942).

Baum, V., *A Tale from Bali*, G. Bles, London (1937).

Belo, J., *Bali: Rangda and Barong. Monographs of the American Ethnological Society*, 16. University of Washington Press, Seattle (1949).

Belo, J., 'A Study of a Balinese Family', in *American Anthropologist, New Series* 38 (1936): 12–31.

Belo, J., *Trance in Bali*, Columbia University Press, New York (1960).

Belo, J., ed., *Traditional Balinese Culture*, Columbia University Press, New York (1970).

Berg, C. C., *De Middeljavaansche historische traditie*, University of Leiden Dissertations, Santpoort (1927).

Berg, C. C., ed., *Kidung Pamancangah, de Geschiedenis van het rijk van Gelgel, Critisch Uitgegeven*, Javaansch-Balische historische geschriften, Santpoort (1929).

Birkelbach, A. W. Jr, 'The Subak Association', in *Indonesia* 16, Ithaca, New York (1973): 153–69.

Boon, J. A., *The Anthropological Romance of Bali 1597–1972: Dynamic perspectives in marriage and caste, politics and religion*, Cambridge University Press, Cambridge (1977).

Van der Broek, H. A., 'Verslag Nopens het Eiland Bali, de Vorsten, Hunne Geaardheid en Betrekkingen, den Handel, de Culture, de Bevolking, Hare Zeden en Gewoonten, Godsdienst en Andere Bijzonderheden', in *Tijdschrift van Oost-Indië* 1 (1835): 158–236.

Covarrubias, M., *Island of Bali*, Knopf. New York (1938).

Van Eck, R. and Liefrinck, F. A., eds., 'Kerta-Sima, of gemeente- en waterschaps- wetten op Bali', in *Tijdschrift von Indische Taal-, Land- en Volkenkunde* 23 (1876): 161–257.

Friederich, R. H. Th., 'An Account of the Island of Bali', in *Journal of the Straits Branch of the Royal Asiatic Society, New Series* 8 (1876): 158–218; 9 (1877): 59–120; 10 (1878): 49–97.

Friederich, R. H. Th., 'De Oesana Bali', in *Tijdschrift voor Nederlandsch Indië* 9 (1847): 245–373.

Friederich, R. H. Th., 'Voorlopig verslag van het eiland Bali', in *Verhandelingen van het (Koninklijk) Bataviaasch Genootschap van Kunsten en Wetenschappen* 22 (1849); 23 (1850).

Galestin, Th. P., *Algemene Kunstgeschiedenis*, vol. 6, *Indonesië*, Utrecht (1951).

Geertz, C., *The Interpretation of Cultures*, Basic Books, New York (1973).

Geertz, C., *Negara: The Theatre State in Nineteenth-Century Bali*, Princeton University Press, Princeton (1980).

Geertz, C., 'Tihingan: A Balinese Village', in *Koertjaraningrat, Villages in Indonesia*, Cornell University Press, Ithaca (1937): 210–243.

Geertz, C., 'The Wet and the Dry: Traditional Irrigation in Bali and Morocco', in *Human Ecology* 1 (1972): 23–29.

Geertz, H. and Geertz, C., *Kinship in Bali*, The University of Chicago Press, Chicago (1975).

Goris, R., 'Secten op Bali', in *Mededeelingen van de Kirtya Liefrinck–Van der Tuuk* 3 (1931): 37–53.

Goris, R. and Dronkers, P. L., *Bali: Atlas kebudajaan, Cults and Customs, Cultuurgeschiedenis in beeld*, Ministry of the Education and Culture of the Republic of Indonesia, Jakarta (1955).

Hadipta, Ida Bagoes Madé, 'Een onderzoek naar de adatstellingen van de desa Buungan', in *Djåwå* 16, no. 1–3 (1936): 102–117.

Hanna, W. A., *Bali Profile: people, events, circumstances (1001–1976)*, American Universities Field Staff, New York (1976).

Helms, L. V. *Pioneering in the Far East and Journeys to California in 1849 and to the White Sea in 1848,*, London (1882).

Holt, C., *Art in Indonesia: Continuities and Change*, Cornell University Press, Ithaca (1967).

Holt, C. and Bateson, G., 'Form and Function of the Dance in Bali', in F. Boas, ed., *The Function of the Dance in Human Society*, Boas School, New York (1944): 46–52.

Hooyer, G. B., *Krijgs Geschiedenis van Nederlandsch Indië*, vols. I–III, The Hague and Batavia (1895–97).

Hooykaas, C., *Cosmogony and Creation in Balinese Tradition*, M. Nijhoff, The Hague (1974).

Hooykaas, C., *Kama and Kala: Materials for the Study of Shadow Theatre in Bali*, Northern Holland Publishing Company, Amsterdam (1973).

Hooykaas, C., *Religion in Bali*, E. J. Brill, Leiden (1973).

Hulsius, L., ed., *Erste Schiffahrt in die Oreintalische Indien*, Hulsius, vol. I–III, Frankfurt (1603).

Hunger, F. W. F., 'Adatuitgaven in Zuid-Bali', in *Koloniale Studien* 21 (1937): 610–640.

Jñānasiddhânta: Secret Lore of the Balinese Śaiva-priest, see: Soebadio, H.

Van der Kaaden, W. F., 'Beschrijving van de Poeri Agoeng te Gianjar', in *Djåwå* 17, no. 5–6 (1937): 392–407.

Kersten, J., *Bali*, De Pilgrim, Eidhoven (1947).

De Klerck, E. S., *History of the Netherlands East Indies*, vols I–II, Brusse, Rotterdam (1938).

Korn, V. E., *Het Adatrecht van Bali*, M. Nijhoff, The Hague (1932).

Krause, B., Bali, vol. I: *Land und Volk*, vol. II: *Tänze, Tempel, Feste*, Folkwang Verlag, Hagen. (1920).

Krom, N. J., *Hindoe-Javaansche Geschiedenis*, M. Nijhoff, The Hague (1931).

Krom, N. J., 'Het Hindoe-Tijdperk', in *Geschiedenis van Neder-landsch Indië*, vol. I, ed. F. W. Stapel: 114–298.

Kusuma, I Gusti Ananda, *Kamus Bali-Indonesia. Kamus Indonesia-Bali*, 2 vols., Denpasar (1956).

Lekkerkerker, C., 'De Baliërs', in *De Volken van Nederlandsch Indië in Monographiën*, Elsevier, Amsterdam (1921).

Liang-shu, *History of the Liang Dynasty*, Chung-Lua Shu-chii, Shanghai, 1929.

Liefrinck, F. A., *Bali en Lombok: Geschriften*, Amsterdam (1927); part of this study translated into English appeared as 'Rice Cultivation in Northern Bali' in *Bali: Further Studies*: 1–73.

McPhee, C., 'The Balinese Wajang Koelit and its Music', in *Djåwå* 16, no. 1–3 (1936): 1–34.

McPhee, C., 'Dance in Bali', in *Dance Index* 7 (1948): 156–207.

McPhee, C., *Music in Bali*, Yale University Press, New Haven (1966).

Mantra Aji Kěmbaṅ, in Hooykaas, C., *Cosmogony and Creation*: 88–91.

Mead, M., *Male and Female: A Study of the Sexes in a Changing World*, Morrow, New York (1949).

Mershon, K. E., *Seven plus Seven: Mysterious Life Rituals in Bali*, Vantage Press, New York (1971).

Mishra, R., *Lintasan Peristiwa Puputan Badung*, Denpasar (1973). *Puputan Badung, Kutipan dan Terjemahan Lontar Bhuwana Winasa* Denpasar (1976).

Nagara-kertagama in Pigeaud, Th. G. Th., *Java in the Fourteenth Century*, vol. III: 1–115.

Neuhaus, H., *Barong* in *Djåwå* 17 no. 5–6 (1937): 230–39.

Pigeaud, Th. G. Th., *Java in the Fourteenth Century: A Study in Cultural History*, vol. I–V, M. Nijhoff, The Hague (1960).

'Purwa Bhūmi Tuwa/Kumūlan' in Hooykaas, C. *Cosmogony and Creation in Balinese Tradition*.

Raka, I Gusti Gde, *Monografi Pulau Bali*, Bagian Publikasi Pusat Djawatan Pertanian Rakjat, Jakarta (1955).

Ramseyer, U., *The Art and Culture of Bali*, Oxford University Press, Oxford (1977).

Rouffaer, G. P. and Ijzerman, J. W., eds., *De Eerste Schipvaart der Nederlanders naar Oost-Indië onder Cornelis de Houtman, 1595–1597*, vol. I–III, M. Nijhoff, The Hague (1915, 1925, 1929).

Sarkar, H. B., *Some Contributions of India to the Ancient Civilization of Indonesia and Malaysia*, Punthi Pustak, Calcutta (1970).

Śiwaratrikalpa of Mpu Tanakuṅ: An Old Javanese poem, its Indian source and Balinese illustrations, translated by A. Teeuw and others, M. Nijhoff, The Hague (1969).

Soebadio, J., ed., *Jñānasiddhânta: Secret Lore of the Balinese Śaiva-priest*, M. Nijhoff, The Hague (1971).

Spies, W. and Goris, R., 'Overzicht van dans en tooneel in Bali', in *Djåwå* 17, no. 5–7 (1937): 205–227.

Stapel, F. W., ed., *Geschiedenis van Nederlandsch Indië*, vol. I–V, J. van den Vondel, Amsterdam (1938–40).

Stutterheim, W. F., *Oudheden van Bali*, vol. I–II, Kirtya Liefrinck Liefrinck-van der Tuuk, Singaraja (1929–30).

Stutterheim, W. F., 'The Meaning of the Hindu-Javanese Caṇḍi' in *Journal of the American Oriental Society* 51, no. 4 (1931): 1–15.

Van der Tuuk, H. N., *Kawi-Balineesch-Nederlandsch woordenboek*, vol. I–IV, Batavia (1897–1912).

Vlekke, B. H. M., *Nusantara: A History of Indonesia*, W. van Hoeve, The Hague and Bandung (1959).

Wittfogel, K., *Oriental Despotism*, Yale University Press, New Haven (1957).

Worsley, P. J., *Babad Buleleng: A Balinese Dynastic Genealogy*, M. Nijhoff, The Hague (1972).

Van Weede, H. M., *Indische Reisherinneringen*, Haarlem (1908).

De Zoete, B. and Spies, W., *Dance and Drama in Bali*, Faber and Faber, London (1938).

INDEX

ACKNOWLEDGMENTS

Werner Forman and the publishers would like to acknowledge the help of the following museums and private collectors in permitting the photography shown on the pages listed:

Denpasar Museum: 16 below, 17, 18 top and below, 23, 26, 28, 73, 81 below, 82 above and below, 87 above, left, and above left, 88 top, centre and below, 117 left and below, 118 below. Dr. L. Goldman, London: 31. Henk Kranenkamp, Rotterdam: Title page, 97 below, 101 above right, 117 above. Museum voor Land- en Volkenkunde, Rotterdam: 120 below.

Werner Forman would also like to thank the following for their help: Dr. H. I. R. Hinzler, Leiden; Madelief Djelantik Hobohm, London; Nyoman Oka, Denpasar; I. Gusti Gde Ngurah Pamecutan, Badung; Wayan Suanda, Denpasar; R. S. Wassing, Rotterdam.